Table of Contents

Introduction 4

Chapter One 7
The GFC Trigger: Mortgage-Backed Securities and CDOs

Chapter Two 21
The Federal Reserve 1999-2007

Chapter Three 28
The Immediate Response 2008

Chapter Four 35
Quantitative Easing: Financial Morphine or Heroin Addiction?

Chapter Five 45
Hi, I'm Japan and I'm a QE Addict

Chapter Six 60
Europe: The Mess That Was

Chapter Seven 69
Europe: The Mess That Is

Chapter Eight 82
The Federal Reserve 2008-2014

Chapter Nine 95
Stock Market

Chapter Ten 104
What We Know Doesn't Work: Credit-Fueled Property Bubbles

Chapter Eleven 111
What We Know Doesn't Work: Countries Loading Up On Government Debt and Old People

Chapter Twelve 123
China: There are asset bubbles . . . and then . . . there's China

Chapter Thirteen 143
Australia: Fool's Paradise

Chapter Fourteen 167
Stock Market Carnage: The Link Between East and West

Chapter Fifteen 175
Recommendations and Concluding Summary

Sources and Recommended Readings 191

INTRODUCTION

The biggest economic disasters always include a credit-fueled property bubble.

Since bottoming out in the 2008 Global Financial Crisis (GFC), the global economy has changed in a big way. The investment community that once possessed a logical mindset that involved buying on the wings of good economic news and selling when bad news hit the headlines transformed into a world where the good news became bad news and bad news became good news for the global markets. More specifically, while the global economy has struggled to find its feet since the GFC, the value of assets across the globe have increased significantly relative to the wages that workers worldwide are paid. This has forced society to invest more but receive less in income.

On the back of rising inequality, the world finds itself in a truly dangerous position. Since 2008, central banks around the world have done what history tells us that central banks should never do—print their way out of trouble. If we look back over time, we see that doing so always ends in disaster. "Printing money" and pumping up the valuation of particular assets in order to create paper wealth against ailing economic trajectories is, in its most simplistic of forms, akin to kicking a can down the road, crossing your fingers, and hoping for the best.

As the global economy took a nosedive in 2008, central bankers, treasuries and political leaders across the globe took what can only be described as a short-term-fix strategy to solve what was essentially a long-brewing problem. The issue at hand back in 2008 was that too much private sector debt was being pumped into the system and focused on a particular asset class. At a certain point, debts en masse could not be repaid, which led to a decrease in available credit across the entre marketplace. This, in turn, led to a house-of-cards moment in the United States, which then spilled into Europe, and ultimately resulted in a global economic meltdown. Previously, all bets had been that real estate prices in the United States would only go up. Unfortunately, many holders of this asset class were burned.

Since this great credit crunch, the global economic and political elite has attempted to defy the common laws of economics by

Print
The Central Bankers' Bubble

Lindsay David

Copyright © Lindsay David 2015

All Rights Reserved

ISBN- 978-1505251357

No Part of this publication may be reproduced, stored in a retrieval system, or transmitted in any form by means of electronic, mechanical, photocopying, recording or otherwise without the prior consent of the author.

To contact Lindsay David please email
lindsaydavidbooks@gmail.com.

Lindsay David can be followed on Twitter
@linzcom

printing money in the hope that global growth will one day simply return and justify the inflated pricing of asset classes where the printed money ended up.

The financial regulators set the rules when it comes to the flow of money. And consistently moving the goal post to cater to what we believe to be a safer economic environment can easily distort the plausible challenges the global economy faces. What do the Basel legislations do to assure that banking systems around the world are protected from calamity? What is considered a risk-weighted asset and what is not? These are among the wealth of questions that might not seem important to the common global citizen, but that is currently the nucleus of the problems that the global economy may have to address, albeit when it is too late.

My greatest fear is that after six long years since the GFC, the world is about to face another crisis that may in fact make the GFC look like a walk in the park. Unfortunately, this time, the problem is simply too out of reach for Main Street to have created it. Enter our central bankers—the individuals in whom we as global citizens are supposed to put our faith and trust that they will make the logical financial decisions to protect the ordinary citizen. It is our central bankers who have created a problem previously unseen by the modern global economy. Furthermore, there are countries and governments that are simply not living within their means.

While American and European households have spent more than the last half of a decade deleveraging, there are now nouveau-riche countries that have adopted the same economic strategy employed by pre-GFC America, Ireland and Spain. Yet these nouveau-riche economies are expecting a different result. Success only lies in the long-term outcome when easy money is involved. Laughing at the economies that took very big hits in 2008 while adopting the very same economic business model makes no sense. But that is the world we live in today. On the back of never-ending Chinese economic growth, the world has forgotten about the common laws of economics and what they preach.

With an excess of money printing and credit still flowing unequally through the global economy, the most powerful bankers—the central bankers—have gotten a generation of institutional investors hooked on the money printing drug, and the addiction is chronic. I fear that mankind will inevitably be left to foot the bill of its actions.

Later in this book, I will make some recommendations that will be tough for central bankers to swallow, but today they are absolutely necessary if we want to build a roadmap to long-term economic sustainability across all corners of the globe. Never should a generation of humanity face another—or worse—economic downturn equivalent to that which was witnessed in 2008.

Chapter One

The GFC Trigger: Mortgage-Backed Securities and CDOs

In October of 2007, the Dow Jones Index peaked at 14,614. By March of 2009, the Dow saw a dismal low of 6,544. In just 18 months the Dow Jones had fallen more than 8000 points on the back of what can only be described as an economic disaster. In the year leading up to the GFC, Americans finally awoke from the delusional belief that the values of their properties would only go higher. The nation that is known for various boom and busts of asset classes once again thought that **this time it was different**. But, as history tells us, when the value of a particular asset class falls out whack (becomes more expensive) relative to income from the long-term historic trend, there is a very good chance that the particular asset class is experiencing a bubble.

What made the American property bubble evident was the way the financial services industry was lending to homebuyers. The bubble was fueled by debt. Homebuyers in 2004 didn't need much to prove that they were able to repay their mortgages. And to be quite frank, until June of 2006 it didn't really matter if you could. Because when property prices rise, lenders take comfort in the fact that even if a homeowner can't pay his mortgage, he can return the keys and the lender will be able to resell the property at a profit relative to what was lent to that homeowner. In the ideal world of 2004, this is what many U.S. mortgage lenders assumed. Not only did the mortgage lenders assume this was the case, the credit rating agencies also assumed this to be the case.

Prior to the bursting of the U.S. property bubble, sub-prime mortgage lenders would lend out money by way of funds collected from Mortgage-Backed Securities (MBSs). MBSs are structured in many ways. The common structure of an MBS consists of multiple investors investing money into the product and, more often than not, they receive the same return on their investments as other investors who have invested in the financial product. A more risky form of funds in the lending market is known as a Collateralized Debt Obligation (CDO)—also known as a Collateralized Mortgage Obligation. In my opinion, a CDO geared towards the housing market back in the mid-2000 era behaved essentially like an MBS on steroids in terms of how you could both invest and profit from it. This was perceived to be a great way for a financial institution to raise money from a diverse clientele relative to the risk-return that was demanded by low- and high-risk investors. There were the hedge funds that were willing to take what I like to call the cheap tranche that offered high risk and high return on investment. On the flipside, there was the ever-so-cautious pension funds seeking safety. And between the high-risk and low-risk investors you had the middle guys looking for a good return on investment, but not to the point where they could lose. This type of financial product generally consisted of consolidated existing loans all packaged up into one single product and sold to investors. Or another method was that funds would initially be raised by the product manager and the resulting raised funds would then be loaned.

I know this sounds a bit confusing at first glance, but take a look at the following table that shows how an investment product is structured in a CDO format.

Investor Type (Tranche)	Money Raised	Stake in CDO	Offered Annual Return on Investment	Interest Owed to Investors	Total Annual Interest paid by Homebuyer
Low Risk	$500,000,000	50%	4%	$20,000,000	$80,000,000.00
Middle Risk- Mezzanine	$300,000,000	30%	7%	$21,000,000	Total Value of the Assets Purchased with Investor Money after 12 months
High Risk	$200,000,000	20%	12%	$24,000,000	$1,150,000,000
Total	$1,000,000,000	100%	6,50%	$65,000,000	

To make more sense out of this table, let's hypothetically say that an investment bank wanted to create a CDO totaling $1 billion. From that $1 billion CDO, the lender wanted to offer interest at a rate of 8% to homebuyers (end users of the funds), and at a higher interest rate if funds were allocated to be lent outside of the property market (e.g., credit card debt). In order for the bank to guarantee that it was able to comfortably raise this type of money to lend to high-risk borrowers, it had to raise funds across multiple investment channels and offer multiple levels of risk to various investors. Also, if you look closely at the table, you will see that there is a $15 million difference between the interest owed to the investors and interest paid by homebuyers. That difference is what was kept by the lender that set up the particular financial product. After paying out a few internal and external commissions (to mortgage brokers), alongside the internal costs of doing business, the lenders would keep the rest as profit. On the other end, banks would collateralize a massive sum of home loans, package them up into a single product, and sell the asset base to investors—and the bank would take a small fee for selling the CDO product. An excellent money maker for what is a slim-margin business . . . *as long as property prices only rise.*

The low-risk CDO investor

Low-risk investors (illustrated in the table)—generally pension/state-managed pension funds and other low-risk investors—seek absolute safety in the investments they make. In return, they accept low returns on their investments, but they have the guarantee that the capital they invest on behalf of their investors will one day be returned. Why did the low-risk investors feel comfortable investing in a lending scheme like a CDO back in 2003? That answer is simple. Three letters. Three "A"s. AAA-rated investment products are what pension funds want. According to rating agencies like Moody's, Standard & Poors (S&P), and Fitch, the low-risk tranche of a CDO was deemed to be fireproof and "safe as houses," because the low-risk tranche was the first tranche to be paid a return once repayments by the pool of homebuyers who borrowed from this CDO came in. Because low-risk fund managers hold such a large pool of the money in this world, it was essential for the banking system to get access to it so that they could generate more business while being able to offer a competitive product to homebuyers. This included sub-prime mortgage lending. So as long as a CDO had a tranche that looked like there was no chance of failure (even if the other tranches could fail), that particular low-risk tranche was given a AAA rating by the rating agencies. When a financial institution's investment product has been stamped with the AAA seal of approval by the rating agencies, the product is a very easy sell to the low-risk investor class.

Many funds out there which manage the retirement savings of millions of people generally demand that the product they invest in be AAA rated. If not, these funds that control trillions of dollars walk away from the opportunity. You will generally find that a responsible pension fund only allocates a very small sum (less than 20%) of the available funds they have for investment into riskier financial products or investments.

The middle-risk CDO investor

Banks selling CDO products need to diversify the risks of the CDOs. Why? Let's say you're lending a total of $1 billion to 5,000 homebuyers; you know at least a handful (1% to 2%) of them are really going to make a mess of their investments over the next decade or two. With this in mind, the banks offer middle- and high-risk seekers an investment that doesn't have a AAA rating. Many fund managers and other investors invest in the middle-risk investor tranche of a CDO in order to gain a larger return on investment, but they still hold what could be regarded as a safe investment, even though it carries a certain element of risk.

The reason the middle-risk tranche carries an element of risk is that, unlike the low-risk tranche, you aren't first in line to receive returns on your investment; but there is still mathematically little chance of not being paid a return. The only way you wouldn't receive a return on your investment is if the CDO allocates debt to a group of property buyers (alongside other debt products outside of mortgages) that actually have no chance of paying off their debts in the midst of a severe economic downturn. But in the heat of the moment in the mid-2000s, it was deemed that property prices were only going to continue to rise quickly and that that would cover any shortfall if a homebuyer was unable to pay down their mortgage, hence, there was an added feeling of a safeguard to this middle-risk investor tranche. There were many funds out there seeking slightly better returns than there were investors seeking AAA-rated returns—and they jumped in on what seemed to be a money-making gravy train.

The high-risk CDO investor

In the mid-2000s, it was the high-risk CDO investors (hedge funds and other investors) who invested in the riskiest tranche of a CDO. They commanded the biggest returns on their investments and allocated sums of money in the tranche that would pay significant dividends—*if* every homebuyer who borrowed money from the particular CDO would repay his debt. And throughout the American property boom, as long as property prices continued to increase year after year, there was a very good chance that even if there were borrowers falling short on their repayments, the lenders who were managing the CDO investments would be able to foreclose on the homes and resell them at a profit.

On the flipside, if mortgage holders who acquired the debts through a CDO struggled to repay their debt obligations in a declining property market, it was the high-risk investors who first failed to receive the anticipated returns on their investments. Using the previous table as a reference, if the hypothetical CDO product only received $58 million (versus an anticipated $80 million) in repayments over a 12-month period, the high-risk tranche would only have $17 million (8.5% return) to share between the investors rather than the anticipated $24 million (12%) return. That in itself is a big hit when you consider that your investment into this product is essentially going to offer you a variable return, but one that is theoretically capped at 12%.

Furthermore, if the asset value of the homebuyers' homes depreciated to a point where it would be deemed impossible for the lender to recoup cash invested by investors of the CDO, it would be the high-risk investors who would first lose their capital. If all high-risk tranche capital is lost, the CDO would then start to drive losses towards the middle-risk tranche investors. And after the middle-risk investors lost out, all would fall on the low-risk investors. But in the mid-2000s, apart from a handful of very skeptical analysts, nobody even considered that any AAA-rated investment that was in the massive list of CDO offerings would ever come close to facing a scenario where low-risk investors would lose out.

Buying high-risk tranches and converting them to low-risk

So if CDOs weren't already confusing enough, you also had asset managers building CDO products by essentially buying into multiple high-risk tranches of various CDOs, packaging them up as their own CDOs, and selling them off to the open market. I like to call this type of CDO a Junk CDO. And like any CDO, Junk CDOs offered different tranches to their investors, with a big difference. These Junk CDOs were full of high-risk tranches from other CDOs; if for one reason or another there was a downturn in the housing market and the high-risk tranches of the CDOs that the particular asset manager had collateralized into his own Junk CDO, the chances of not getting any returns whatsoever on investment become very high. Yet product managers were still able to get AAA ratings for the top tranches of the Junk CDOs.

How did the CDO business model break down?

The business model broke down when it became evident that the U.S. property market was receding and the high-risk tranches of CDOs would not be paid any returns. Therefore, this meant that the Junk CDOs en masse would receive absolutely no returns whatsoever, leaving AAA-rated investors with nothing.

As long as U.S. property prices continued to rise, investors in all tranches of a particular CDO were able to receive the healthy returns on investment that they were originally seeking with minimal risks. This is what the business model of a tranche-split CDO depended on to continue to stimulate new money from potential investors—money that could then be invested into new offerings that the lenders (both prime and sub-prime) were presenting to the market. However, if either property prices began to drop or mortgage holders en masse began to struggle to repay their debts, the mathematical inevitability was that the business model of the MBSs on steroids, particularly the Junk CDOs, would break down, starting with the lenders who had the riskiest client profiles. The end result was what is known as a House of Cards moment.

During the U.S. property boom years, the banking system had a very lucrative moneymaker on its hands. CDOs were coming out of every crevice of Wall Street and being sold to investors of all risk appetites worldwide. To make matters worse, Junk CDOs were now flooding the market, and because the ratings agencies were giving the top tranches of these Junk CDOs an AAA rating, pension funds were confidently jumping in and investing. In the eyes of the MBSs providers, the investors, and the mortgage holders, the business model was regarded as an all-around safe investment to make. This was despite the obvious risky possibility that mortgage holders may not be able to pay back their debts. Investors were so confident in the lending products at the particular point in time that many would even leverage their capital investments with debt to invest into a CDO so that they were able to multiply their profits.

Imagine that you own a hedge fund and you have $10 million to invest in a high-risk CDO tranche, but you want more returns than the annual $1.2 million (12%) you anticipate on receiving over the lifetime of the investment. What do you do? You go and acquire some debt so that you can increase your stake in the CDO investment. Back in the mid-2000s, hedge funds could take their $10 million and raise sums of debt that now simply wouldn't be allowed. But let's just say your hedge fund acquires $80 million in debt to invest in the CDO high-risk tranche. With $80 million in debt plus $10 million of the capital from the fund, you now have a total of $90 million to invest into a particular CDO.

Now, the bank wants to charge you 7% annual interest for the money that the hedge fund has borrowed. But if the annual yield from the high-risk CDO tranche seems all but certain to give fire-safe returns, the fund on an annual basis will receive $1.2 million for the first $10 million invested, plus another $9.6 million from the debt the fund used to increase the size of its investment into the product. In sum, you will have a return of $10.8 million. Deduct the 7% ($5.6 million) that the fund has to pay in interest on $80 million, and the fund will be left with a very handsome $5.2 million (52%) annual return on a $10 million capital investment. And back in 2004, such a move by a hedge fund would have been deemed a conservative investment when compared to some of the leverage multiples that were actually taken on by investors for this purpose during this era.

Now, if this hedge fund (that invested $90 million with only $10 million capital and $80 million debt) was caught in a CDO investment that could only offer 5% return to high-risk investors, the hedge fund would have a big problem. With $5.6 million owed in interest, a return of only $4.5 million from the CDO would mean that the hedge fund would lose money. Even worse, if the investment was made in a junk CDO, the hedge fund would soon be extinct.

As we know, this moneymaking MBSs/CDOs party finally came to a very abrupt halt. When it became apparent that the prices of U.S. properties couldn't rise any higher, the mother of all downturns began before the mainstream media could even grasp a hint of the scenario that would eventually unfold. As property prices stalled in 2006, there were many investors still rushing to invest in the MBSs money machine. But there was a problem. The large amount of Americans who now had new homes and new mortgages meant fewer buyers available for lenders to give as much debt to in comparison to the previous year. Eventually, the sub-prime lenders that were lending MBSs/CDOs-raised funds to homebuyers were forced to find new homebuyers on the back of a property market leveling off. Unfortunately for the MBSs, there were simply not enough buyers willing to take on new sums of debt. Not only did demand for property dry up because of the sheer prices of real estate relative to what households were earning in income, but property purchasers were no longer willing to pay more for a property than a purchaser was willing to pay 12 months prior. Then in June of 2006, prices stalled for a few months and started to head south—and it became clear that the high-risk tranche investors of many of the CDO products would be in trouble, more specifically, the investors who had leveraged their investments to multiply profits. And on the back of all this, the Junk CDO investors were all but doomed. The result? Millions of investors around the world lost their retirement savings.

So, on the front end of this collapse in lending were the mortgage holders who were losing their jobs and struggling to pay their debts in a moment when property prices were beginning to recede. On the back end were the hedge funds that were going bust because they too could not pay back the debts that they had acquired to invest in the high-risk tranches of CDOs. Furthermore, so many pension funds were getting burned from investing in AAA-rated tranches of Junk CDOs that they withdrew from investing—this withdrawal created a global credit crunch.

Once the flow of money was interrupted on both the front and back ends of the MBSs products in play, there simply was less money available to lend to homebuyers. This was deeply problematic in a market system that was 100% dependent on lenders lending more money to new homebuyers than the amount that was loaned to the previous homebuyers. The property market went as far as it could go and then the business model broke down. Who wants to invest in any type of MBS when property prices are crashing and hedge funds everywhere are getting burned? This essentially broke the wheel of a business model that shared a similar risk profile to a PONZI scheme. I call it the IZNOP business model *(which I will explain in another chapter)*—and all who'd invested in MBSs wanted out. It became impossible for investors to recoup their investments. Hence, in 2007, bad news was the norm and investors in all tranches of a CDO were finding themselves unable to recoup their investments.

The Wealth Effect

As property prices continued to climb in the United States, Americans who owned a home began to feel wealthier. Imagine you earn $45,000 yearly and live in your own Miami home that you purchased for $180,000 in 1997. Just eight years later the home is worth close to $400,000—and you feel a lot richer. Even though the price appreciation in the value of your home continues, it doesn't mean you have an extra $220,000 that magically ends up sitting in the bank. Far from it! But still you feel much wealthier. However, there's a big problem with the wealth effect when it comes to asset price appreciation. Because you feel wealthier and look wealthier on paper, you become comfortable borrowing against your new paper wealth. You borrow money to buy a nicer car, buy an investment property, or invest in the stock market.

The big problem with the wealth effect when it comes to the value of the home you own, or invest in, is that buying and selling real estate is essentially a zero-sum game. Just because your house and the land your house sits on is appreciating in value, doesn't mean that the value of every other house on your street and neighborhood is not going to do the same. So essentially, the only way to reap the full benefit of an appreciating asset (your house) in a particular asset class (your neighborhood) is to sell the asset and walk away altogether from reinvesting in that particular asset class. If you do not walk away from reinvesting your money into the same particular asset class you profited from, you are essentially selling your inflated asset to purchase another inflated asset. And more often than not, you acquire more risk to do so to improve your standard of living.

In late 2005, the banking system had no problem lending money to homeowners, because lenders had construed that this new paper wealth would provide a buffer in a mortgage holder's ability to pay down a mortgage. Let's say the value of the home you own in Miami is worth $400,000 in 2005. You only have $90,000 of debt left to repay on the mortgage you took on when you initially purchased your house for $180,000 back in 1997. Because the U.S. banking system is happy to lend to you, you decide to upgrade your living conditions (buy a nicer house in a better neighborhood). So what do you do? You sell your existing home for $400,000, and then purchase a $600,000 house. In order to pay for the upgrade of living standards, you have to borrow $200,000 to cover the $200,000 shortfall in funds, leaving a total debt burden of $290,000 to repay once you include the $90,000 from your initial mortgage. On a $45,000 salary, there's a good chance 60% of your income is now going toward mortgage repayments. As you are now allocating a large chunk of your salary to repay your debts, you are forced to tighten your spending belt elsewhere. Furthermore, your risk profile increases significantly—so much so that you are now essentially living paycheck to paycheck while the value of your new home increases. Property prices in Miami are skyrocketing, and as long as you still hold your job and the price appreciation of the property exceeds your loan repayments, you are becoming richer—on paper.

However, if property prices in Miami were to decline or you were to lose your job, you would find yourself with a very big problem which—when multiplied with multiple homeowners—would break down the entire lending system.

The collapse of the Wealth Effect

First, although you're feeling wealthier, you're keeping less cash in your pocket week after week. You're also now pumping less money into the broader American economy outside of the housing industry because you're spending more in debt repayments. Imagine that millions of Americans across the nation are in the exact same situation as you, and they en masse are also not able to spend as much in the shops and on their lifestyles.

This was the situation leading up to the 2006 property market downturn. To make matters worse, there was a barrage of first-time homebuyers who had been lent exceptionally risky sums of debt relative to what they earned annually. For a homebuyer, 100% financing was accessible in most of the American states. And when there is crazy money flying around, there is always someone crazy enough to borrow it.

A large proportion of Americans were spending a greater percentage of their 2006 incomes on debt repayments and less in the real economy—thus was the beginning of the end of the "easy money" era in the United States. Why? Fewer Americans spending outside of the housing market means less revenue for retailers and other service providers. If there's less money flying around, there's less revenue and profit generated by businesses. This squeeze on revenue forces businesses to reduce their number of employees—and it is all but certain that a healthy proportion of the new jobless are responsible for mortgages. If you were caught up in the wealth effect and you lost your job, you found out very quickly that you weren't that rich after all. In fact, you were holding significant sums of debt, and in most cases you had to sell your home to cover the losses you were incurring from mortgage repayments. And that was the trigger that sent the American economy into a tailspin.

By 2007, the American property market had cooled from its June 2006 peak. Because Americans now needed a significant chunk of debt to purchase a home relative to what they were earning, this price moderation, and eventual downturn, was a very clear signal that less money was being lent to homebuyers than the previous year. And with the median house price across the United States peaking at 4.6x(times) median household income, there was a lot of room to fall if the median price returned to its long-term historic trend of somewhere between 2.7x and 3x incomes.

As for the hypothetical situation in Miami: if you lost your job in March of 2007, you had quite a problem on your hands. First, you'd upgraded your living conditions through the use of debt. And because you'd been living paycheck to paycheck before you'd lost your job, you had very little alternative but to sell your house to pay off your mortgage. Even though you'd managed to pay down $15,000 in principal since the purchase of the $600,000 home, you still had $275,000 in principal to pay back to the lender on top of the interest. At the same time, though, there were also other new homebuyers (who'd acquired 100% financing from lenders) also losing their jobs and being forced to sell their homes. As there was clearly less investor money being pumped into MBSs, there was less money to lend, which meant that property owners across America were being forced to take a haircut on the sale price.

Selling homeowners had to compete against a wealth of other homeowners looking to sell their homes in order to get out of their financial problems. This led to an influx supply of properties available on the market relative to the existing demand. In the Miami example, this left homeowners very confused. Over the previous several years, the newspapers had always reported that Miami was suffering from a chronic housing shortage. This shortage of housing coupled with a growing population was supposed to suppress any risk to the local real estate market.

Unfortunately, this housing shortage, like most housing shortages, turned out to be just a myth that had been overshadowed by an oversupply of debt to homebuyers in the lead-up to 2007. Similarly, this caused house prices to fall across the majority of property markets in America, where an oversupply of mortgage debt had significantly fueled the rising price of property. And the cities and towns that had the fastest rise in property prices relative to the median household income took the hardest hits. Residents of California, Florida, Arizona, and Nevada were notable victims of this credit-fueled property bubble. The business model of the U.S. real estate market broke down—and this triggered the largest economic meltdown in the United States since The Great Depression.

The collapse of AAA-rated CDO investments

As the entire lending system in America broke down, real estate prices plummeted and foreclosure rates shot through the roof. Due to rising foreclosures, practically all CDO investment products went unspared. Hence, they didn't earn enough money in interest to pay back all investors in all the tranches.

While the previous table illustrates how the different tranches of a CDO were paid in good times, the table below is an illustration of what eventually became the reality of some of these CDOs, following the collapse of the American housing market. As Junk CDOs were dependent on income derived from the high-risk tranche of a CDO, without income, their AAA-rated tranche would become worthless.

Investor Type (Tranche)	Money Raised	Stake in CDO	Offered Annual Return on Investment	Interest Paid to Investors	Total Annual Interest Paid by Homebuyers
Low Risk	$500,000,000	50%	4%	$20,000,000	$30,000,000
Middle Risk-Mezzanine	$300,000,000	30%	7%	$10,000,000	Total Value of the Assets Purchased with Investor Money after 12 months
High Risk	$200,000,000	20%	12%	$0	$600,000,000
Total	$1,000,000,000	100%	6,50%	$30,000,000	

In the table above, in terms of the value of the assets held by this hypothetical CDO, there is now a $400 million shortfall. On top of this, because there was only $30 million in interest paid by mortgage holders, and investors in the low-risk tranche are the first to be paid ($20 million), the investors in the middle-risk (*receiving $10 million instead of $21 million*) and high-risk tranche (*receiving $0 million instead of $24 million*) are taking a double hit by losing income whilst the value of the assets their invested funds were used as debt have depreciated in value. $1 billion was raised, but the assets that the fund invested in are now worth only $600 million.

If the CDO has to pay its low-risk investors $20 million in interest and return the money that those investors originally invested, mathematically it would be near impossible in a falling housing market to recoup the funds needed to cover the low-risk investors' AAA-rated investment in a Junk CDO, according to the investment contract. Any AAA-rated investment opportunity generally offers the investors the right to pull out their money whenever they please. Any AAA-rated product that doesn't have a break clause in an investment should never be rated AAA.

What is clear in the above table is that the high-risk tranche investors are getting no returns. Therefore, the Junk CDOs would get back nothing in total for all investors. This is where the Junk CDO market collapsed. As for some mid-risk investors of a CDO, they unfortunately got burned just like the Junk CDO investors. In its most simplistic form, if the CDO operators were not able to sell a property to recoup funds, they could not repay the investment made. So much for AAA-rated products!

Chapter Two

The Federal Reserve 1999-2007

Alan Greenspan was the Chairman of the United States Federal Reserve (the Fed) from 1987 to 2006. Throughout his time as chairman, he and his colleagues saw a lot of economic ups and downs and would react accordingly by raising or lowering the interest rate based on economic fundamentals, unemployment, shocks, and bubbles. Greenspan, arguably one of the most respected central bankers of all time, was consistently shifting interest rates up and down for all sorts of reasons when compared to the two Federal Reserve chairs who would follow in his footsteps, Ben Bernanke and Janet Yellen.

When you look at how interest rates in America moved up and down between 1999 and 2007, you can see that there was a central bank lifting and lowering interest rates to accommodate solid growth while shifting interest rates higher to mediate growth and inflation. And in emergency situations, the Fed would take strong measures to protect the American economy from possible disaster. As the dot-com boom was peaking, the U.S. economy was moving forward with growth of over 4% on an annual basis—a very strong growth rate for an established economy. The interest rate in October of 2000 was at 6.5%. Interest rates had been slowly rising in the U.S. as a result of the Fed trying to cool off the investment frenzy into technology stocks. Furthermore, inflation in the U.S. was on the rise and heading towards 4%. The dot-com bubble was simply an out-of-control investment plunge into a particular asset class that was delivering minimal yields relative to the asset value of the majority of publically listed technology companies. Essentially, it was a market that didn't really care what a particular technology stock was selling or wanting to do. As long as the name of the entity ended in ".com," there were grossly more investors wanting to own that particular stock rather than sell it, thus driving up the valuations of some companies which had absolutely no revenue and no real profit-generating business model.

As interest rates began to moderate growth and investment in technology stocks cooled off, the Fed reduced interest rates in accordance to promote growth and moderate a slowing economy while defusing the technology bubble on the NASDAQ. By the end of January 2001, the Fed had shaved 1% off of the interest rate, bringing it down to 5.5%. By March 2001, America had entered a very mild (but non-technical) recession. And by August 2001, the interest rate was at just 3.5%. So, by August of 2001 the NASDAQ had returned to a more reasonable level. In fact, the NASDAQ fell incredibly in line, returning towards its long-term growth trend.

In my opinion, this was a very well-managed interest rate cycle that the Fed and its leader, Mr. Greenspan, had implemented. The dot-com bubble was massive, so much so that it took Wall Street by storm. With gradual tightening, however, the Fed achieved its objective. While the unemployment rate had moved between 3.8% and 4.1% in 2000, it had climbed up to 4.9% by August of 2001. It is not an easy task to get rid of the dot-com bubble, slow things down a little, and allow investors and the economy to regroup while not driving the economy into a technical recession (with two consecutive quarters of negative growth). With just one quarter of negative GDP growth (-1.1%) by March of 2001, the economy swiftly readjusted, and it was back to building on the fundamentals by the next quarter, growing by 2.1%. It was then anticipated that there would be a clear rebalancing act with growth in the third quarter being less than the previous 2.1% growth. But by then the world had changed.

Nobody could ever have predicted the events of September 11, 2001. The Fed immediately responded by bringing the interest rate down another 1% to 2.5% to stem the inevitable shock to the American economy. While America was preparing for war, it certainly proved its economic resilience. After a -1.1% decline in GDP in the first quarter of 2001 and a 2.1% rebound in the second quarter, America's GDP dropped by just -1.3%.

In 2002 and 2003, the American economy was still readjusting from the end of the dot-com bubble and September 11th. In order to boost growth and put a lid on unemployment, which was slowly on the rise, the Fed continued to reduce the interest rate all the way down to just 1% by June of 2003 when unemployment peaked at 6.3% before recovering gradually throughout the remainder of 2003.

The Hidden Killer

Looking back at the Fed's American monetary policy between 1999 and 2003, what is very clear is that it took proactive measures to curb the dot-com bubble and it raised interest rates until investors began easing up on buying stocks that generated no income. On the flip side, the Fed responded to an emergency and helped stop America from falling into what could have been a deep recession following September 11th. On the back of all this rode the real estate market. Between 1987 and 1999, property prices had all but remained fairly flat relative to incomes. But by 2003, the U.S. property market was really bucking a trend. Property prices in America were rising consistently, although it was understandable why this fact wasn't initially picked up by the Fed's radar. Between 1999 and 2003, the median property price in the U.S. grew by 5.6%, 5%, 3.6%, 6.9%, and 4.3%, respectively. When compounded, that equates to 27.8% total growth in property prices from the beginning of 1999 to the end of 2003. And by 2004, following another 13.3% rise in the median property price, Americans were paying 45% more for real estate than they had been just six years earlier.

So, what became very clear was that as one overinflated asset class was deflating (dot-com), money was being invested into another asset class, inflating *its* value and cost to purchase. More particularly, it was an asset class that everyone in a civilized society needs. A home. And as property prices across America were rising, so too (in sync) was household debt—and this was all happening along with increasing investment into the structured financial products within the very financial system that was allowing Americans to obtain greater access to debt. This debt was pumped into America's heartland, as well as into coastal states with high population growth such as Florida and California. Cities like Miami and Los Angeles were the most notable cities to experience frenzy-like spikes in the price of real estate.

If I had been Alan Greenspan back in 2002 and I was trying to manage one problem after another, I would have wanted to hear some good news from time to time. And at face value, rising property prices was good news because it promised to spur construction activities that would cover the shortfalls of an economy that, for a short period of time, had stalled as the "regroup and start again" phase was at its peak.

What also made it harder for the Fed to recognize the credit-fueled property bubble that was brewing was that real estate in the United States was much cheaper and much more affordable than it was in most real estate markets in the Western world. Before real estate prices in the United States took off, the median house price-to-income ratio was roughly around 3x the household income. In other words, if the median household income in the United States was $50,000, the median price of property would be $150,000. When compared to other countries with property markets that shared some common characteristics both by city design structures and city density, American real estate in 2001 looked like a very good deal. Both Canada and Australia, though with weaker currencies at the time, had their citizens paying a higher price for real estate relative to what they were earning alongside higher interest rates.

So, as property prices and household debt in the United States continued to climb relative to incomes, property prices started costing 4x the median household income in and around 2004. But in the states where more debt was being pumped, property prices were growing at a much faster rate relative to what the local residents were earning. In 2004, the median house price in America had spiked by 13.3%, meaning that after 12 months with interest rates at 1%, the American economy had rebounded. And every time that the Fed board met from June of 2004 to June of 2006, interest rates in the United States rose by 0.25% to curb rising house prices, rising household debt, and the rising stock market. Even Hurricane Katrina in 2005 didn't slow the Fed's tightening policy. By June of 2006, interest rates had peaked at 5.25%. Then in February of 2006, Alan Greenspan left office and Ben Bernanke took over as Chairman of the Fed, and it seemed like Greenspan had left at just the right time—leaving a big mess for the new guy. Bernanke was forced to follow Greenspan's tightening policy until June of 2006, creating much calm before a very big storm.

Continuously raising the interest rate by 0.25% was simply not enough to stop the credit-fueled property frenzy that eventually unfolded. In just a handful of years, Miami's median house price went from a norm of 4x the household income up to 7x by the peak of the American property bubble. Los Angeles went nuts as median house prices rose from the city's 6x-income norm to over 11x. In the Northeastern region of the U.S., including New York and Boston, prices rose versus the median, but they grew nowhere near as fast as did the prices in the Western or Southeastern regions of the country. A slower rise in property prices in the Northeastern U.S. and Texas mediated the true national situation at hand for the Fed. Slower house price growth in these regions stopped the national data from looking too out of whack. This consolidation of data essentially hid how nuts the credit-fueled property and construction boom actually was in certain regions of America.

As the Fed was increasing the interest rate over and over again, property buyers were forced to pay more interest. And new homebuyers in 2005 and 2006 took on bigger mortgages than did property buyers of previous years—complete with these higher interest rates. It was clear that the constant pressure asserted by The Fed would one day kick in and pull back house prices. But economic bubbles are generally much harder to tame than anticipated. And the fact that the Fed didn't rein in the credit-fueled property bubble earlier was probably the biggest mistake in modern American economic history. As property prices began to level off in 2005 and into 2006, America had an unavoidable challenge on its hands. Those who were warning about a U.S. housing crash went largely ignored. However, they would soon see their predictions become reality.

With interest rates at 5.25% and the average interest repayment on a mortgage much higher, the Fed had the mother of all problems. Because so many Americans were now paying so much of their income on all this new housing debt and funneling less into the mainstream economy, an unstable fault line was created that would essentially bring the American economy to its knees. In just eight short years, household debt-to-income ratio in the United States went from the equivalent of 90% of annual household income in debt to more than 120% by the peak of the American property bubble. The Fed's biggest mistake from 1999 to 2007 was that it didn't recognize early on in the property boom that household debt was spiraling out of control. By the time that Alan Greenspan and the Fed put two and two together and identified a dangerous trend of house prices and debt being in sync and rising at a rapid rate, it was simply too late. However, the eventual reaction by the Fed did, in fact, stop the madness. Unfortunately, the warnings from the Fed were largely ignored by a population that was hell-bent on being in the property game. Society, and the institutions that lent societal members the debt, became married to the belief that property prices would only rise. But by 2007, America realized that this was no longer the case. And policymakers at the Fed had to wipe a lot more sweat from their foreheads.

As the property price declines accelerated across the United States, it was only then that Americans realized the mess they'd got themselves into. Never could the Fed have fathomed such a worst-case scenario occurring. When you have massive levels of new and toxic debt entering a particular asset class, tough and immediate measures must be taken in order to stop a credit-fueled disaster from happening.

The end of an era

In my opinion, 2007 marked the end of an era when common sense had prevailed without the American government and Federal Reserve going above and beyond their roles and means as economic managers. The Fed, though usually a bit late to identify asset bubbles, was ready to pull up their sleeves and make a concerted attempt to cool down an asset class and economy by raising interest rates and heating up the market and economy when it looked like it was sailing into the doldrums. When interest rate cycles are cyclic, there will always be a governing tool down the road that can be utilized in both good and bad times. Over the last 45 years (prior to 2007), U.S. interest rates have never flatlined. In fact, interest rates have continuously risen and fallen according to the economic conditions at any particular point in time. A lot has happened since 1971. Oil shortages, wars, cold wars, the collapse of the Japanese economy—not to mention a few stock market crashes.

Just as important, the Fed had as good an example as any of what happens to an economy that flatlines when there is too much leverage in the system and the bubble bursts, and then the government gets too involved in trying to pick the economy off the ground through artificial means. This example was the collapse of the Japanese economy in the early 1990s. So in a moment of economic calamity, the Fed ended an era of common sense and entered a new era of madness by driving interest rates down to a nonsensically low level. By the end of 2007, interest rates were on their way down from their peak.

When it comes to economics, history has an excellent track record of repeating itself. Asset bubbles rise, a population becomes delusional and thinks that "this time it's different" in a "too good to be true" moment—and then the bubble bursts. This is what history tells us. And as economic hell broke loose in the year following 2007, the Fed, along with the U.S. government, essentially adopted almost the same recovery model that has a good historical track record of not working out so well—not only for the economy in question, but for those who manage it. On top of all this, the Fed became no longer just a manager of the economy, it became an investing participant for years down the road.

Chapter Three

The Immediate Response 2008

By the end of 2007, it was becoming very clear that the U.S. economy was in big trouble and recession was just around the corner. MBSs products were dead and flanked by rising oil prices. In other words, not only were American property prices tumbling, but the spike in the price of fuel relentlessly peaked at over $140 per barrel in 2008 before finally nose diving along with the rest of the American economy. This did not help the financial services sector one bit!

By early 2008, investment bank Bear Sterns was acquired for cents on the dollar. By September 2008, hell broke loose when it was clear that Lehman Brothers was all but certain to go bankrupt if there was no bailout or acquisition. Alongside Lehman, you had some of the biggest home lenders—Freddie Mac and Fannie Mae—also in no-win situations. Countless large and small companies in the United States could not gain access to the credit needed to keep business chugging along. If there was ever a moment when the world's largest, most innovative and dynamic economy was at risk of being sent into oblivion, September of 2008 was it.

The moment when Lehman fell into bankruptcy was the tipping point for the global economy. The global business model had essentially broken down, and there would be no light at the end of the tunnel unless governments and central banks around the world stepped in to either cover hemorrhaging losses or pump money into their economies and banking systems to soften what would eventually be the mother of all knockout blows. In the hours following the collapse of Lehman Brothers, the world, for the first time, truly realized in amazement how interconnected the global economy actually was. There had simply been no other event in modern history (neither good or bad) that had confirmed so categorically that the global economy was . . . global.

I was in New York on a business trip in September of 2008. I will never forget the shocked faces I saw on the day Lehman collapsed. A grown man in a suit walked past me on a busy Midtown Manhattan street openly weeping. The city was steaming with shock and awe. In mid-2007 it would have been almost impossible to find a soul who would've thought that Lehman Brothers would collapse before October 2008. But Lehman Brothers did collapse. And the global economy was completely caught off guard.

When it became increasingly clear that Lehman would falter, the U.S. Treasury made a last-ditch attempt to find an acquirer of the firm. The British bank Barclays took a good look at this deal, but when a big bank from one country wants to acquire a big imperiled foreign bank, there are serious red-tape and regulatory challenges to pass through. And, essentially, the British government did not want Barclays to absorb a toxic asset. The deal fell through and Lehman filed for bankruptcy.

In the pit of this moment of calamity, systemic risk across the global banking system was a given. Now that one major global investment firm had collapsed, the global economy was choking on the fact that the flow of money around the globe had essentially stopped and the asset value of planet Earth was dwindling by the minute. Unless governments and central banks worldwide stepped in and made a bailout, investment, or stimulus of some sort, trillions of dollars within the banking system would be stuck between a rock and a hard place for far too long while the value of global assets continued to depreciate, reducing the difference between how much money was owed in debt versus the asset valuation of the assets that held debt. For every realized dollar that a bank was losing, it had to take a dollar out of its own bank account to cover the loss. Millions of U.S. households holding mortgages under water is one thing, but a drowning global economy is another. And that was where the world was heading.

Following the collapse of Lehman, it was immediately evident to the American Treasury and Federal Reserve that they had to step in to soften the blow. And other countries had no choice but to follow suit to prevent a rush of money from one financial jurisdiction to another. Furthermore, stock markets across the world were tumbling. The assets on the balance sheet of Lehman

Brothers were equivalent to **5% of American Gross Domestic Product.** That alone puts the scale of the problem into perspective.

The U.S. government's response to the threat of a systemic implosion of the global banking system was the Troubled Assets Relief Program (TARP). TARP was essentially a $700 billion bailout/rescue/put-a-brick-wall-in-front-of-systemic-risk package that was set up by the federal government to purchase MBSs and other junk in the U.S. financial system that were causing this global credit crunch so that money would once again be able to circulate throughout the American economy. The world's largest insurance company, American International Group (AIG), was also insolvent. It cost American taxpayers $182 billion to bailout AIG. AIG going completely bust would have exponentially worsened the problem at hand. The U.S. government also acquired some of the financial institutions that failed, such as Freddie Mac and Fannie Mae. TARP's money was also used to buy preferred stock in banks, to bailout insurance companies, to buy toxic debt . . . and the list just goes on. But this illustrates how many aspects of a broken-down business model had to be fixed to prevent the knock-on effect that could break down the whole global economic system.

The economic blow to the United States was so severe that it punctured a hole right through the very heart of the American economy. Even after the TARP bailout, all of the economic problems that America had were not resolved overnight. On the back of TARP, the Fed stepped up from its ordinary role and began to build its balance sheet using quantitative easing measures. Furthermore, America was not the only country with a government agency injecting massive amounts of cash to save its economy.

Europe

When the banking system in the world's largest individual economy became lodged between a rock and a hard place, the flow of money was affected in all other continents beyond North America. What had been triggered in America was now simultaneously impacting Europe on a large scale. Spain and Ireland were experiencing massive credit-fueled property bubbles of their own. Furthermore, the London property bubble and financial system were also imploding. The world also became more aware of the heavy government debt burdens held by countries such as Greece and Italy. In my opinion, the number or economic weaknesses exposed over the failure of a single investment bank is simply incredible. Even the economies of Germany and France took beatings. And banks all over Europe required immediate cash injections to survive.

The big challenge for Europe was that it was the not only the biggest economic downturn for decades, but it was the first major economic downturn since the introduction of the euro currency. Europe is comprised of many different countries, all with different cultures and ways of handling economic crises. But they were all now bound by a single central bank and a single currency. The Italians must have been kicking themselves. Italy no longer had the option of printing the Lira to weaken it so much that it created inflation, thus driving down debt while stimulating exports and kicking the "debt can" down the road to a future generation.

Just like the United States, Europe was forced to put a brick wall around its own banking system to protect it from this systemic financial collapse. More than 1.3 trillion euros was committed by E.U. member states to fight this systemic invasion from mauling its overleveraged banking system. Meanwhile, the United Kingdom's government all but nationalized the Royal Bank of Scotland and Lloyds Bank by acquiring a greater-than-50% ownership to stop those institutions from falling down the same fatal rabbit hole that had swallowed Lehman Brothers.

Countries across Europe were simply stunned. Even the all-mighty Swiss were shocked. The Swiss bank UBS had to get a government-backed bailout to the tune of $59.2 billion. That is a hefty price tag for a country with a GDP of $450 billion back in 2008. To really hammer the seriousness of the moment home, UBS had always been recognized as the safest bank in the world. The crisis was overwhelming.

China

In 2007, China's GDP was growing as fast as 13%. By 2009, China's GDP had dropped all the way down to 6.2%. If only the West had had this hyper-growth problem. But the reality is that prior to this economic slowdown, China was already constructing infrastructure and housing at a stifling rate.

As the can of economic worms opened up in Europe, China was trying to grapple with the slowdown in trade which in turn had led to a deceleration in the country's overall economy. While the western hemisphere was contending with the credit crunch, China was in the midst of a construction binge. How else can you consistently have such hyper-growth? Furthermore, China was also extremely dependent on exports. As the world sourced more affordable manufacturing, China had established a well-oiled and ever-improving supply chain wherein global companies could have their products manufactured in China and exported to their country of choice for sale.

When the ripple effects of the credit crunch fell on China's doorstep, on November 9, 2008, China produced the mother of all stimulus packages—$586 billion—to stop its GDP growth from dropping below 6%. This stimulus package was no bailout. It was quite simply a cash injection into the economy to build more infrastructure and housing on top of what it had already been building. In terms of global economics, the impact that this news had on commodities sent sighs of relief across the countries that were essentially 100% dependent on China continuing its chronic construction binge.

Japan

If I had been the Japanese Prime Minister in late September of 2008, I would have called the President of the United States and leaders across the European Union and said "Welcome to the Club!." Japan's economy was already in recession by the time Lehman Brothers had collapsed. But the big impact that the credit crunch had on Japan was more trade related than fiscal. Keep in mind that for years prior to the GFC, Japan had been unsuccessfully trying to fully recover from the effects of its own economic breakdown in the late '80s and early '90s. The deleveraging event that Japan experienced in that era was the biggest the developed world had witnessed prior to the U.S. credit crunch.

In 2008, trade between Japan and its trading partners in emerging Asia almost came to a grinding halt, dropping by more than 50%. That's a big hit, if you consider that more than 50% of Japan's exports went to emerging Asia. On top of that, exports to the United States and Europe fell by roughly the same figure.

And, unlike most currencies, the global financial meltdown strengthened the Japanese yen, which was a contributing factor to the sharp downturn in export value in yen terms. On June 7, 2007, USD$1 got you ¥123.40. By Christmas of 2008 USD$1 got you a just over ¥90. In 2008, Japanese government debt to GDP was already standing at 167%. This was by far the last thing Japan needed. But, unfortunately, being the exporting nation that it is, it took one large punch to its already bruised stomach.

Although on paper Japan felt the immediate pain of this sharp economic slowdown, it must be said that Japan has tried time and time again to get the economic engine rolling, albeit with no success. And in 2008, for the "umpteenth" time, Japan launched yet another stimulus (printing money) package—$275 billion. And for the "umpteenth" time the country saw another recession not long after.

The commodity club of nations

If you lived in a commodity-producing nation and exporting natural resources to China was the backbone of your economy, back in 2008 you could consider yourself lucky because you pretty much avoided most of the heavy pain and suffering that was experienced in the United States and Europe. When China launched its massive stimulus, iron ore producers in countries like Australia, Brazil, and nations in Africa were relatively spared from this global economic tsunami. Oil-rich states in the Middle East and Latin America also thanked their lucky stars. If you were a strategy consultant assessing the growth model of China back in 2008 and you were trying to figure out how long this boom would last for resource-rich nations, you could be mathematically all but certain that China would absorb any new supply of mined and refined resources that could be extracted from the ground until the year 2012. Although most commodity-producing nations experienced recession during the GFC, the punch to the guts was nowhere near as hard.

Another interesting response that must be noted came from Australia. Prior to the realization that China would be the savior of its economy (which was marching towards recession), the Australian government gave taxpayers $1,000 to go and spend in the economy. And Australian's did just that. They injected the money back into the system from the bottom up. In my opinion, this was a very successful strategy that worked to save an already highly leveraged private sector. Had it not been for China implementing its stimulus plan, Australia was all but certain to find itself in a deep recession where one of the most chronically leveraged property markets in the world would have had no alternative but to deleverage. This could have made the American credit-fueled property bubble bust look like a trot in the park, as I will explain in another chapter.

So, in response to the bad news from the United States and Europe, the Reserve Bank of Australia slashed interest rates. If any western country or economic union did not fall into recession back in 2008, it was because the economy of that country or union was as closely linked to China as was Australia's economy. Nothing else! But by the end of 2008, and with great cockiness, Australian's gladly nominated themselves for, and bestowed upon themselves, the award for having the smartest economists in the world. Luck will do that!

The foundation of today's reality

So, in summary, the immediate responses from governments and central banks around the world were to fend off a global systemic risk to the global banking system alongside China launching the most ambitious infrastructure binge in history. At a cost of trillions of dollars, the initial response by global central bankers only scratched the surface of the troubles that would lie ahead.

It was becoming very clear that the initial response by the global economy would simply not be enough to get rid of all the structural challenges that had been a long time in the making. And as most citizens in the northern hemisphere would now have to get used to living with less access to debt, it was becoming very clear in the eyes of the most powerful central bankers in the world that more needed to be done to stave off the risks of deflation and to get the global economy back in motion. When it comes to interest rates, the decisions made following the initial response by central banks and governments worldwide would inevitably lead the global economy into what I like to call the "Interest-Rate Flatline Era."

Chapter Four

Quantitative Easing Financial Morphine or Heroin Addiction?

Quantitative Easing (QE) is generally a last defense "if all else fails" tool used by a country's central bank in an attempt to stall or slow an economy from experiencing a harder downturn than what would have been suffered without intervention.

Essentially, when a central bank employs QE, it prints money with the intent to reduce the economic burden in an already troubled time and use the printed money in various ways. For example, if there's a credit crunch and there's not enough cash flying around in a particular economy, the printed money will be used to purchase the particular assets from a financial system that's threatening to stall the flow of money. The result? Freeing the blockages that prevent the flow of money so money can begin to comfortably circulate again throughout an economy.

QE is an exceptionally powerful tool. More commonly than not, QE will generally raise the valuation of a particular asset or debt that a central bank purchases or invests in, and that brings down the yield, or repayment. In theory, this should ultimately force a banking system to distribute money to a particular part of the economy where there is a lack of available funds (e.g., credit). Let's use Treasury bonds (government debt) for example. The main reason that yields from Treasury bonds in the U.S. and most jurisdictions in Europe are as low as they are today versus the long-term historic norm is that the respected central banks are purchasing these bonds at a price that makes the repayments of the bond (interest) much lower than they would be if all bonds were freely sold to the open market in the midst of a severe economic downturn. This can help the government to reduce its interest burden while making this particular asset class less attractive to investors, which theoretically would be persuasive enough to make investors put their money elsewhere (i.e., where there is not enough lending). If QE helps to reduce the government debt burden by allowing the government more access to affordable debt while reducing its weekly or monthly repayments, then it is perceived that it will help to boost the economy and the flow of money through the economy. This is normally (in theory) achieved on the basis that pumping printed money into the system creates inflation, thus artificially boosting GDP while interest rates are at a rock-bottom rate.

As a hypothetical example regarding the effects of QE, let's say that Country A has a GDP of $100 billion and is in the midst of experiencing a financial recession. Moreover, Country A's government has debt equivalent to 100% of GDP ($100 billion). The stock market index in Country A peaked at 1,000 points before heading south during the recession, and it has now fallen to 600 points. Furthermore, Country A's currency, for one reason or another, remains historically strong against major international currencies.

Because the economy of Country A is now in recession and the government already has the equivalent of $100 billion in debt, a contraction of the economy of, let's say, -0.5% in the next quarter would mean that Country A would then hold $100 billion in debt in an economy with a GDP of $99.5 billion. If the repayments of the bonds offered by the government of Country A are costing the government 10% a year in interest, for every 10 dollars spent within the economy, one dollar would need to be taken out of the economy and used by the government to repay interest. On top of that, the banking system in Country A would probably be simply too nervous to lend money to businesses and individuals, so the banks would keep their money in Treasury bonds.

Therefore, in order for Country A to reduce its government debt burden and get the banking system lending to the private sector, the country's central bank would have to step in and reduce interest rates to near zero and assist the nation in the reduction of its debt burden and access to credit through artificial means. This would include printing money and using it specifically to purchase new Treasury bonds at an inflated price to reduce the yield (interest) the government would have to pay in order to keep more money circulating within the economy of Country A. Furthermore, this policy would probably make banks think twice before investing in Treasury bonds, as the yields are too low when compared to the yields that could be made lending to the private sector.

If, for example, Country A's central bank purchases $3 billion in new Treasury bonds at a yield rate of 1% and this is used to pay back the other bondholders' interest alongside the government spending more money on productivity within the economy, there's less risk that Country A's government won't be able to pay its debts. So essentially as other Treasury bonds that Country A issued in the past reach maturity, they slowly reduce their annual debt repayment burden on the back of low interest rates. However, more than likely, this strategy would increase the overall amount of government debt owed. But on the flipside, this monetary easing would be expected to create inflation while interest payable is at a minimum.

In addition to Country A's central bank printing money to purchase government bonds in a near-zero-interest-rate environment, the government also recognizes that its stock market index is taking a big beating. Since Country A fell into recession, the local stock market index has dropped by 40%. To instill confidence in the market, the central bank may decide to print money in order to purchase stocks to reduce further sell-offs. Accordingly, the central bank prints a further $2 billion to purchase stocks in various ways (e.g., preferred stock), thus providing assurance that the central bank will make all attempts to prevent the stock market from falling any further. Let's face it, if you know a central bank is going to print a ton of money and that money is going to be used in one way or another to buy stocks, you can comfortably make the assumption that the stocks in the particular index will rise.

As mentioned, the prime intention of the central bank in Country A is to help money flow smoothly and evenly throughout its economy by enticing banks to lend while the central bank is artificially making the yields in particular asset classes poor.

In an ideal world, this is how printing money in a recessionary environment is used as a short-term tool by central banks to protect stock markets, bonds, and the value of other assets from falling too far, while prodding the banks to lend to the private sector to get the real economy moving forward. Artificially alleviating pain in the market while creating inflated assets to scare away investors should theoretically all but certainly get banks to allocate money to the private sector. But on the flipside, QE is a very high-risk financial tool if not used properly. The ramifications of failing to properly administer such a stimulus can lead to an awful eventual scenario wherein QE could eventually cause significantly more pain in the long term than the short term relief QE is intended to provide an economy.

The difference between a shot of morphine and addiction to heroin

Imagine an ambulance arrives at a hospital carrying a man who is suffering several shattered bones in his arms and legs after being hit by a car. The patient is in excruciating pain. A doctor immediately gives the patient an injection of morphine to take away the severe pain and offer relief. As the doctors examine him, they know that this patient has a big problem. To assure that the shattered bones are able to recover and re-form to the way they were prior to the accident, he will need urgent surgery wherein metal plates and screws will be placed in his arms and legs. The doctor and his team take the patient in for surgery. However, the pain the patient wakes with after such intricate and intense surgery is more unbearable than the pain he experienced when he was hit by the car. So the doctors administer a constant but temporary dose of morphine in the patient's drip to consistently stop him from experiencing severe pain. After a few days of rest and morphine, the body starts to heal from the accident and the surgery. After three days, the doctors begin to reduce the patient's dose of morphine as the level of pain is now less severe. And after six days, the doctors discontinue the use of morphine as the pain in the patient's arms and legs is now manageable.

As the pain from this surgery is now manageable, the patient's body is essentially healing from the accident and surgery. To fully recover, the patient will have to rest many months and do no activities that could bump or cause pain to his arms and legs. As the patient recovers, day-by-day he starts to feel better. Slowly but surely, he is able to use his arms and legs. After many months, he is able to go back to a normal life where he can stand on his own two feet without pain.

As this example shows, the morphine was used and administered in a very responsible manner at the moment the patient needed morphine most to alleviate what would have been an unbearable situation. It was *not* used throughout the whole recovery process. Imagine breaking your arms and legs, getting rushed to hospital, going through surgery only to wake up with metal plates screwed into your bones. To go through several days of treacherous pain would simply be unbearable without morphine. In this modern period, it is normal that morphine would be used to alleviate the immediate suffering. But as the body heals and the patient begins to have less pain, the use of morphine should also be decreased and then discontinued as soon as it is clear that the patient will not experience pain above a certain threshold. To do otherwise and continue the use of morphine would be to risk making the patient addicted to the drug—and creating an entirely different yet equally serious problem.

Like the responsible administration of morphine by doctors, central bankers strongly consider administering such a tool as QE in a moment when the pain in the economy is becoming completely unbearable. And QE, like morphine, will provide a short period of much-needed relief from the pain an economy is suffering. While printed money is being circulated in the system, it buys the economy time to fix its problems before the central bankers take away the powerful pain-killing tool. Responsible use of QE means that it is used only at a moment of absolute pain and then it is withdrawn to allow the economy to stand on its two feet and go through the normal ups and downs of a recovery. But when QE is not administered properly, the end result can lead to an economic catastrophe that can cause more problems than the problem a central bank was trying to solve in the first place.

From a shot of morphine to heroin addiction

The risks of QE going out of control can be easily compared to an individual who becomes addicted to heroin following the responsible administration of morphine following an accident. Let's take a new look at the previous hypothetical situation. As previously, the patient who was hit by a car enters the hospital, gets a shot of morphine to alleviate the pain, and goes through the surgery to get metal plates and screws put into his arms and legs. After the surgery, the patient receives morphine for a few days, and then the doctors say he no longer needs morphine to reduce the pain as the pain is now well below the patient's tolerable threshold. But as the patient has become accustomed to feeling pain-free, the new lack of morphine in his bloodstream leaves him feeling a disagreeable level of pain. He finds it very irritating. He asks the doctor if he can have some morphine to lower the pain he is feeling while his body heals. So the doctor, being a lot more flexible than he should be, agrees to give the patient a little more morphine to keep him from feeling any pain at all. The problem now is that the patient's body has become more accustomed to morphine, so to get rid of the lower level of pain he's experiencing, he still requires the same dose that he needed immediately after his emergency surgery.

The patient's becoming very comfortable with morphine in his bloodstream. Perhaps he's also liking the feeling. It makes him feel better, but it *does not make his bones stronger* so that he can one day walk on his own two feet again. What the patient doesn't understand is that morphine will not heal his body. All morphine does is alleviate pain. And when the patient returns home after two weeks in hospital, he has no more morphine. The closest drug that will offer the same relief as morphine is heroin. As the patient is now impatient with the pain (manageable pain) and addicted to the feeling of being pain-free, he looks for relief. Through shady connections, he obtains and starts to take heroin. Like morphine, heroin does absolutely no good to the human body. It's very addictive, and after just a few hits of the heroin, the patient is now even more hooked. In fact, to get the same feeling, he requires more heroin than he did for the previous hit. If he doesn't have a regular hit of the drug, he starts to feel bad. And his bank account runs dry because he has this expensive new habit that offers absolutely no returns. So the patient starts to sell his assets. After that, he panics and sells his television, getting relief after another hit of heroin. Unless he walks away from the drug altogether, he risks losing everything because he's so hooked that he needs more and more of the substance in every hit he takes. And he wants to use it for every little bit of pain he gets. Even if it's the slightest headache, he wants to take more heroin—until the inevitable when he takes too big a dose and his heartbeat flatlines.

An overdose of QE can have the same fatal effects to an economy as heroin does to humans. If QE is not administered properly, investors prefer to invest where the printed money ends up in order to ride the rise in the asset price in the name of capital gain. For example, if a central bank prints money to buy bonds and stocks for the next 12 months, investors would rather buy stocks and bonds than lend to the private sector. If the central bank buys stocks, it commonly raises the stock valuations of publically listed companies. But when the central bank retreats from purchasing stocks, the market becomes spooked and could send the stock market valuations down. The investors' addiction to profiting from QE is so high that if the central bank stops purchasing particular assets that the investors bought (because the central bank was buying them), the investors will rush out of the market . . . unless the central bank gets spooked regarding the ramifications of walking away from purchasing assets. Thus the central bank feels pressure to keep buying assets of the particular asset class where investors followed the central bank in the first place. And to achieve the same result every time the central bank pumps printed money into a particular asset class, the bank has to inevitably print more than it did the previous time to achieve the same results. So more often than not, each time investors get worried, the amount that the central bank has to print and invest grows.

Let's again visit Country A

As Country A's stock index fell from a high of 1,000 points down to 600 points, Country A's central bank began a QE program, investing in stocks and bonds to allow the market to regain its composure, level off, and head back up. The price-to-earnings ratio (P/E ratio) of stocks when the index was at 600 points was 10x earnings. That is, for every dollar a company on the stock market earned in profit, the company was valued at 10 times what it was earning on an annual basis.

In this scenario, Country A's central bank prints $2 billion to purchase stocks over the next 12 months. Investors jump onboard and invest in the stock markets as the central bank buys stocks, and Country A's stock market index rises 200 points to a high of 800 points over the 12-month period. That's a 30% increase in the valuation of the stock market in just one year. But when it becomes inherently clear that QE will soon come to an end, investors get spooked about keeping their money in a stock market and they start to pull their money out. This causes a pullback on the market, bringing the stock market index down to 730 points.

This 10% drop in the market now spooks the central bank. So, in order to try to instill confidence once again in the stock market, the central bank prints another $2 billion and administers another round of QE. Like the first time around, investors rush in to buy stocks, and the market not only recovers, but the stock market roars past the 800-point mark all the way up to 1,000 points. That's a 25% increase from the previous year's peak of 800 points. Country A's investors are loving their central bank and the money it's pouring into the stock market that they have twice invested in! But the P/E ratio of stocks in the market is now back up to 15x earnings. This means that stocks are not offering as good a return on investment when compared to a year earlier. But investors don't care because they're making a fortune in capital gains. All of the investors' concerns about the fundamentals of the companies on the stock market have been pretty much thrown out the window. They don't care anymore about the performances of the companies they have invested in; they're more concerned about whether the central bank will print more money and buy more stocks! But after 12 months of a second round of QE, investors become less nervous that the central bank will walk away from investing in a third round of QE.

Then Country A's central bank says that they won't offer a third around of QE. This spooks the investors again and they begin to withdraw their funds from the stock market, bringing the stock market index in Country A back to 910 points. And once again Country A's central bankers become concerned that the market will inevitably crash if they don't continue to invest in the stock market. So the central bank caves in and invests $2 billion more into stocks. And once again stocks climb. This time the index rises to 1,200 points. That's a 20% increase from the previous year's peak of 1,000 points. Each time the same amount of money is used to buy stocks, it has less effect in percentage terms.

As you can see, the investors are more easily spooked when a central bank seeks to retract a tool that it used to relieve the pain in the worst-case scenario (rather than help drive investors to score an easy dollar). Investors become so addicted to the easy money that they rush en masse into the market when QE is implemented, and they want to back out when the central bank retreats from investing in the stock market. And although the QE program is initially used as a shot of morphine to provide a temporary relief from a very painful moment, the market gets hooked on the QE drug and the central bank ends up providing a continuous supply of the QE drug in the same way a drug dealer supplies heroin. Each time Country A's central bank prints and pumps money into the stock market, growth declines in terms of percentage gains. So, while the first QE stimulus increases the market valuation of the stock market by 30%, stock value only grows by 20% by the third round of QE. The only way to create increased value and growth in percentage terms would be if the central bank was to increase its investment into the stock market each time it printed and pumped money. Otherwise, you end up with less punch for the same amount of printed money. If this strategy of printing and pumping is undertaken for too long, it simply breaks down, and any money printed becomes worthless. In other words, using QE as anything beyond a one-off relief injection generally never ends well.

Psychologically, Country A's central bank has been far more than accommodating. As for Country A's investors, why would they deploy their cash to lend to the private sector when, instead, they could take full advantage of a no-brainer way to make easy money? The ultimate end of this story is that the investors got hooked on the ease of making money, and the central bank lost its backbone and caved into the investor community by continuing to pump easy money into the system. The end result is that 1) Country A has a stock market that is completely overvalued with P/E ratios that don't make any sense to mom and pop investors, 2) a banking system that didn't lend to the private sector as much as the central bank wanted, and 3) an investor base so hooked on QE that it will begin to cost the central bank more and more printed money every time that investors kick and scream. In other words, the country has a market that makes no sense and the end result is that the particular inflated asset class that received the injections of the central bank's printed money has one very big fallout when the central bank is forced to stop QE. And just like the heroin addict who overdoses, the particular financial market collapses. Moreover, because there was limited lending to the private sector by the banking system, the economy of Country A is still far from a full recovery.

Now that we know the pros, the cons, and the risks of adopting a QE program, we can use this chapter as a guide to see how QE has been utilized by actual countries over recent history and how most of these cases have ended up in failure. And the best example is a country that had a shot of morphine that turned into a lifetime addiction with poor results.

Chapter Five

Hi, I'm Japan and I'm a QE Addict

At the outset, it must be said that when a country spends more than 22 years attempting time and time again the same failed strategy to get itself out of an economic mess, one would imagine that someone within the Bank of Japan's (BOJ) strategy department would be forced to face the conclusion that what the BOJ is attempting to do again and again and again DOES NOT WORK!

The debt spree

When we examine what caused Japan's economic crisis of the early 1990s, one thing is very clear. When there is too much debt in an economy and it goes unmanaged by a central bank for too long, the result is the mother of all economic disasters. In the lead-up to Japan's economic downturn, the country, its corporate sector, and its citizens were showering themselves with easy credit in a frenzy that is stunning to look back upon.

Between 1983 and 1991:

- Property prices in Japan rose by an astonishing 150%. Almost all that growth occurred between 1986 and 1990. And it wasn't the price of houses that was rising, it was the actual land. *While property prices rose by 150%, land prices rose by more than 200% in some cities.*

- Commercial property prices in most major cities rose by at least 250%, while commercial rent rose by roughly 100%.

- The Nikkei stock market index rose from 9900 in 1984 to peak at **38,957** on December 29, 1989.

By all mathematical accounts, there can be only one culprit for such an astronomical skyrocket in property prices coupled with such high valuation of publically listed companies in so short of a time frame. That culprit was DEBT! In the late 1980s, the Japanese lost all sense of reality. The argument back then was that there was not enough land or housing in Japan, thus the property prices were going up and up and up! This was the argument made by the banks and those with a stake in real estate, and it was held up as the justification as to why property prices were rising so fast. Corporations across Japan became bigger and were scaling up operations like there was no tomorrow. So how on earth could the value of Japan's assets rise so fast without debt? It couldn't!

The sheer scale of this bewildering delusional madness was something the modern world had not really seen before. Yes, Japan was pioneering in the field of electronics and had become an exporting powerhouse. But domestically, the Japanese were essentially caught up in a debt frenzy and access to credit was cheap and easy. Japanese would outbid each other to get their hands on a piece of land. So while the banking system was freely lending money to homebuyers, they were also telling the homebuyers that there was a shortage of land, thus property prices would only continue to increase faster than what borrowers' debt repayments would be.

The credit-fueled property bubble

In 1985, the median house price in Japan was 5.7x the median household income. By 1989 it was 7.4x income. Property prices continued to soar into 1990 before stalling and collapsing like a fly with an exploding heart.

Why did Japanese property prices skyrocket between 1985 and 1990? If you believed the Japanese banks that were lending all the money to homebuyers, land prices were rising so fast because of an apparent shortage of land coupled with a sharp increase in the number of people seeking to purchase real estate. Japan has 836 inhabitants per square mile, so one could say that the banks had a very good point. Due to the country's high density, the price per square meter (m2) of land should theoretically be higher relative to income than it is in a country like Australia where there are only seven people per square mile.

The metropolitan Tokyo area has 30 million+ residents, which translates into 6,810 inhabitants per square mile over a 5,240 square mile area versus Sydney's 380 inhabitants per square mile (4.7 million people in roughly the same area). Because of this, we could expect, relative to incomes, the residents of Tokyo to pay a higher price per m2 of real estate than the amount a Sydneysider would pay. And in the 1980s/early '90s, the residents of Tokyo were fighting each other tooth and nail to get their hands on real estate.

So the median house price in central Tokyo rose to an astounding 18x incomes. Even the greater metropolitan area of Tokyo nudged past 10x at the peak of the bubble. And that number can only have been higher when data is broken down suburb by suburb. But when you ventured into the outer suburbs of Tokyo, prices, though still high, would depreciate significantly. Overall, however, the property bubble in Japan was widespread, with Tokyo and other major Japanese cities leading the charge. In today's money, Tokyo's property prices peaked at over $1million in 1990. A quarter of a century later, the median house price in Tokyo is valued at a measly $311,000. That's a big plunge.

As property prices were skyrocketing, this land shortage argument was clearly overshadowing what was the true reasoning for rising property prices and the unusually high demand for real estate in what was a very unaffordable housing market. *Access to credit.* This was similar to what happened in the United States at the height of its housing bubble, whereby the belief that there was an actual shortage of land or housing stock in cities like Miami and Los Angeles masked the massive oversupply of debt available to homebuyers. The problem that the two countries experienced was essentially the same. *Powerful people with invested interests were telling society that property prices were going to rise due to overwhelming demand. The reality, however, was that massive sums of debt were piled into a particular asset class (real estate). That's what was stimulating demand in what would have otherwise been a very unaffordable market.* In a nutshell, household debt relative to the size of Japan's GDP rose by more than 40% on the back of what was essentially a property market that was not based on fundamentals, but on speculation in pursuit of capital gain. And the banking system was lending more to homebuyers than it had the previous year, creating the ability to purchase housing that otherwise would have been out of reach for the absolute majority of homebuyers.

Credit-fueled corporate and banking sector

Japan's credit-fueled spending spree extended well beyond the real estate market. Firstly, the banking sector supplied abnormal sums of credit to both the housing and business sectors. Secondly, Japan's banking system went from having a debt profile equivalent to 45% of the total GDP in 1980 to upwards of 119% of the total GDP in 1990. In other words, Japan's banking system became 2.64x more leveraged relative to the size of the Japanese economy in just a 10-year period. By any measure, this is an extraordinary shift in such a short period of time. On the back of this, Japan's corporate sector debt grew from 108% of the GDP to 147% of the GDP over the same decade.

By all accounts, Japan's rapid accumulation of debt was piled into assets. And as there was so much artificial money flying around the Japanese economy, the Japanese started to go on spending sprees by spending the capital gains made. Any Japanese person who was a grown adult in the 1980s will tell you how flash cars, fine whisky, and expensive watches were must-haves. The executives at the major Japanese corporations were living the dream. The stock valuations of Japanese companies were rising faster than anyone could ever have imagined. The P/E ratio of the stock valuation on the Nikkei 225 made it to as high as 55x earnings. That's an unthinkable number in an upswing economy. In other words, for every dollar invested into a Nikkei 225 stock, you would expect earnings to be a measly 1.8% on an annual basis. That's not a good market to be in when hunting for dividends. So, in the same way that the Japanese property market was in pure speculation mode, so was the stock market. Let's face it, it would be very hard to live off your retirement fund without digging into its capital if you were only receiving less than a 1.8% return—hardly any of which would end up as an actual dividend.

Essentially the Japanese went from living off fundamentals to living off capital gain created by a chronic expansion of credit. As for those who stayed out of the mad asset-buying rat race in a nation that had the mother of all asset bubbles? They were left behind . . . until 1991.

When you look at a historical P/E ratio chart of the Nikkei 225 between 1980 and 1992 (more particularly between 1986 and 1991), you see how the P/E ratio shot up into the atmosphere and then got shot down. The chart doesn't even look like it has a mountain. It looks like a slightly bumpy road heading towards a 20-mile-high mountain only to fall off the backside of this large mountain. Compare the P/E ratio chart to the Nikkei 225 index chart and you will see that the rush of madness was ultimately doomed for disaster. Unless more debt was pumped into an already overleveraged corporate sector, it was all but mathematically certain that the publically listed companies in Japan would be comprised of nothing but an overvalued and under-delivering asset class relative to the stock market valuation of each and every company in Japan.

Then reality kicks in

In the lead-up to the beginning of the end of Japan's economic miracle, it became very apparent that the banking system was struggling to lend more to the private sector than they'd already been doing throughout the '80s. By the early '90s it was very clear to the Japanese that there was no housing shortage, and furthermore that there was no economic miracle. There were only businesses, banks and households that now had balance sheets that were screaming one word: DEBT! The reality was that the island nation of Japan was using toxic sums of credit to build a future economy that was mathematically never going to exist in the first place. Talk about one astounding slap to the face!

Let's face it, in the mid-late 1980s there were even some economists predicting that Japan would one day overtake the United States to become the world's largest economy! After the end of the World War II in 1945, Japan was one big disaster zone. After years fighting a lost war, the country was in absolute ruins. There was no shortage of land back in 1945, but there was a shortage of food. It cost Japan and the Allied Forces a fortune to get Japan back standing on its own two feet. Fast forward 40 years and this country was one of the three most technologically advanced economy's in the world. From the late 1940s following the end of World War II until the peak of this economic boom of the 1980s, the Japanese worked hard to gain the international respect the country deserved—only to lose a lot of that respect when reality finally set in. Japan was experiencing what could only be described as a once-in-a-century bubble that would shake the very heart of what is a very proud nation.

The BOJ super asset bubble burst

How did the cost of assets in Japan reach such screaming heights? There is a pretty clear indication that the Bank of Japan simply allowed them to and did nothing about it until it was far too late. Interest rates between January of 1987 and January of 1989 were at a long-term low of 2.5%. Compare this to the 9% rate of just several years earlier and it's clear that there were all the hallmarks indicating that credit could easily flood the Japanese economy. While interest rates were at 2.5%, the Nikkei 225 index went out of control, rising without anything blocking its path. As the Nikkei continued to climb into January of 1989, the BOJ finally realized that it was forced to raise interest rates to try and cool off a stock market that was the most out of control in the developed world. Finally, by May of 1989 the BOJ raised the interest rate to 3.25%. That's a 0.75% rise in one single hit—something not seen very often at all. But then the BOJ didn't make any further rate changes until October of 1989, when they jacked the interest rate up another 0.5% to 3.75%. Still, after a 1.25% rise in interest rates, the Nikkei 225 index was still climbing at a rapid rate. So, in December 1989, the BOJ added another 0.5% of interest to raise the interest rate to 4.25%. And in December of 1989, the Nikkei 225 index reached its stunning peak of 38,957. But for the Nikkei 225 index, it was all an extraordinary, down-hill swan dive to the end of the road from there.

Now that the stock market was heading south, the BOJ still had to resolve the credit-fueled property bubble—which was not showing too many signs of deflating. While one asset class (stocks) was tumbling very fast, property was not. Over the course of a few months, the BOJ incremented the interest rate to 6%, which was enough to diffuse the Japanese property bubble. And by 1991, the property market started to drop rather swiftly. Before you knew it, Japan's economy began to look like one big gigantic mess full of toxic asset that held liabilities worth more than the actual value of the asset.

As Japan's private sector was deleveraging, there were few tools available for the BOJ to ease what was a crumbling private-sector economy. At that point in time, the best approach available was to reverse interest rates and send them southward. But when arguably the greatest credit-fueled asset bubble in modern history is bursting, a country finds it near impossible to fathom in the early stages of the bursting that the price of assets across the board will return to the long-term historic trend. Imagine property investors in central Tokyo buying real estate at 18x incomes and saying "property prices won't go down that far!." Why would a property investor say that? Because that investor has lost touch with reality! When reality does kick in, how could an investor react if he or she had taken on a mortgage for an unaffordable property so they could one day flip it for a higher price—but the market bursts? Imagine if you were one of those property buyers who lost 70% of the value of your asset after the Japanese property bubble burst and you still owed the bank 50% of what you paid for the property almost a quarter-century ago? This is the reality for many Japanese today!

When the private sector and, more particularly, homebuyers take on as much leverage as the Japanese did in the late 1980s/early 90s it doesn't matter how fast you bring interest rates down. When you break the highly leveraged IZNOP *(Ponzi spelt backwards)* business model down, you will always witness a mass exodus from a particular market.

The IZNOP business model

As house prices were rising across Japan, the Japanese real estate market got caught up in what I like to call the IZNOP business model. Although not at all an illegal Ponzi scheme, the IZNOP business model shares incredibly similar characteristics to the risk-profile of a Ponzi scheme. For those of you unfamiliar with the Ponzi scheme, according to the U.S. Securities and Exchange Commission, it is:

> *An investment fraud that involves the payment of purported returns to existing investors from funds contributed by new investors. Ponzi schemes require a consistent flow of money from new investors to continue. Ponzi schemes tend to collapse when it becomes difficult to recruit new investors or when a large number of investors ask to cash out.*

Like a Ponzi scheme, when there is a large amount of debt in a particular asset class, the value of the asset class increases according to the increase of credit being pumped into that particular asset class. But if the banking system either cannot, or is not willing to, pump more money into that particular asset class year after year, there is simply no other place for the valuation of a particular asset class to go but down. And like Ponzi schemes, IZNOP business models either grow or breakdown.

Furthermore, if buyers begin to think that an asset class requires significant amounts of debt to acquire relative to their incomes and they walk away from the market en masse, this too also breaks down the IZNOP business model. Alternatively, in a low-interest-rate environment, if property buyers take on massive sums of debt only to be hit with higher interest rates, this too can breakdown the IZNOP business model. Rising unemployment is another key model breaker. In other words, like a Ponzi scheme, the IZNOP business model simply has absolutely no margin for error and depends on more debt in both sum and income ratios being pumped into the particular market than was previously injected.

Imagine if back in 1988 the median property for sale in Nagano, Japan, hypothetically cost $300,000. If the median household income in Nagano at the time was $30,000, the price of property would be 10x the median annual household income of the city's residents. It would be all but mathematically impossible to generically save $300,000 for the median household in Nagano. But if the banking system is willing to lend the median household in Nagano $260,000 as long as the household can come up with the other $40,000, home ownership is possible for the median Nagano household. And if multiple homebuyers are all fighting each other to get their hands on a piece of the Nagano dream because there is so much debt flying around, the banking system is creating artificial demand because its flexible lending standards allow so many homebuyers the ability to purchase homes that would otherwise be financially out of reach.

If 12 months later the banks in Nagano were willing to lend $320,000 to the median homebuyer—depending on if there are enough people out there crazy enough to take on this type of debt relative to what they earn—property prices should have theoretically risen by $60,000 (20%).

But if we had fast-forwarded 12 months later and the banking system was only able to lend $200,000, as compared to the

$260,000 it was loaning out a year earlier to a median income homebuyer, do you think that property prices in Nagano would have risen? The banks would lend $60,000 less (versus the year before) in a housing market dependent on debt to cover the difference between the amount of their own money that homebuyers can spend versus the sale price—so, in theory, the median property price should decline by $60,000 leaving a median house price of $240,000 (-20%). This means those who purchased a property the year before when it cost $300,000 would now be holding a mortgage underwater and still have interest payments to make. Essentially, when property prices at a certain point reach well beyond affordability in a particular jurisdiction, and the market is more dependent on the banking system lending more debt year in and year out to homebuyers, the market is caught up in an IZNOP business model. And when you factor in human instinct, nobody wants to purchase property in a market that's falling fast while still needing massive sums of debt to make a purchase.

There is only one way that a particular property market can become so far out of reach for homebuyers unless they take on excessive sums of debt. That is when a very significant proportion of wealthy, cash-paying property buyers from another region or country are all buying property in a particular area. This is what has happened in a handful of neighborhoods in a handful of cities across the globe (e.g., central London, Manhattan and Monaco). Today, these expensive property markets are more dependent on wealthy individuals to purchase real estate than they are on homebuyers who take on massive debt. But unlike in central London or Manhattan, foreign property buyers didn't make up a large proportion of property buyers anywhere in Japan during the peak of that country's property bubble. So while ever-increasing leverage ratios caused the Japanese property bubble to rise to the heights it did, they also brought the market crashing down once the IZNOP business model had broken down. Then, the painful deleveraging process began.

In my opinion, there is no greater risk to an economy than a property market being caught up in an IZNOP business model. A property purchase is the largest investment that the majority of households in any country will make. This means that when a property market is caught up in an IZNOP business model, there is very little room for error. Once a negative trigger hits a particular property market, it is doomed to take a very big drop.

Practically every square meter of the Japanese property market was caught up in the IZNOP business model, so when that model broke down and interest rates rose, Japan was left with large numbers of property owners who held debts that were all but unpayable. And the country is still today paying the ultimate price for adopting the IZNOP business model.

But the Japanese thought printing money could solve everything!

It was becoming very clear following the collapse of the housing market that lowering interest rates was not enough to provide a buffer against an IZNOP business model gone bad. The Japanese economy was going to experience a prolonged era of deleveraging while government debt was bound to rise. And between 1988 and 2014, government debt relative to GDP has climbed from the equivalent of 70% of GDP to 227% of GDP! It seems that this country simply can't live within its own means! On the back of this guaranteed deleveraging event, Japan had already gone through a very important demographic transition. As Harry Dent rightly points out in his book *The Demographic Cliff*, Japan also had an aging population that had already peaked and passed its prime purchasing power days. On top of this, the country had a near-0% population growth and was heading towards negative population growth. These factors, as Harry Dent suggests, would not help Japan one bit in its recovery. As the country has fewer people at working age, there will generally be less productivity and spending. But even with this challenge arising in Japan, the alarm bells simply did not ring. So by the late 1980s, there was no strategy developed by the Japanese government nor the BOJ to facilitate such a shift in Japanese demographics, which still today has yet to be seriously addressed.

In the late 1980s, Japanese policy makers had essentially two choices to make in what is one of the most important moments in Japanese economic history. Those two choices were either to:

1. Embrace a pro-immigration policy, or
2. Embrace and build an economic model around a declining population.

As the asset bubble was bursting, it became critical for Japan to adopt either of these two strategies. If Japan wanted an economy that could produce organic economic growth, it needed more people. With a declining birth rate, the only way this could be achieved is by opening the country to immigrants from around the world to increase its population. On the flipside, if Japan had embraced the fact that it was all but inevitable that its population would decline, Japan needed to shift the wealth and higher-paid jobs from the older generation to the younger generations of Japanese so they would continue to spend in a deflationary environment. This would make younger Japanese couples financially comfortable enough to financially support raising more than one child. And more critically, the cost of assets simply had to be very affordable for the older generation, and there had to be a reasonable cost of housing alongside more attractive P/E ratios on the stock market, allowing for far better yields on investment.

Unfortunately, a quarter of a century later, the Japanese have adopted neither strategy. The strategy that the Japanese government and BOJ *did* adopt left the Land of the Rising Sun with a problem that may never go away.

Print the Yen

There were two very reasonable options on the table to structurally improve Japan's domestic economy based on the demographic situation; so why on earth did Japan not adopt one or both of these policies? The main reason Japan adopted neither approach was that the country's central bankers and politicians tried to take the easy way out of what was, and still is, a very big problem.

In 1991, Japan's chief response in its attempts to alleviate the massive deleveraging process was to reduce interest rates and bail out what industries it could. Over the next four years, under the guidance of the BOJ governor Yasushi Mieno, the BOJ brought the interest rate all the way down to 0.5%. This did nothing to curb the deflationary pressures in play. And by the end of the 1990s, the BOJ had brought the interest rate to 0%. What did this do to help the Japanese economy? Nothing.

In 1998, the BOJ was given no alternative but to recapitalize the Japanese banking system, which was simply undercapitalized and, as a whole, unable to withstand the continuous influx of non-performing loans. Interest rates were at 0%! The banking system simply could not stand on its own two feet. Smaller institutions were crumbling. Trillions of yen were printed to stop the banking system from getting into worse shape than it already was. This did stop the economic bleeding, but the wound created by the burst asset bubble simply would not heal. Even though the banking system had received a government-paid capital injection, the Japanese economy was still flatlining like its interest rate.

The consumer price index in Japan has remained all but flat from 1993 until today, 2014. *That is 21 years of no price growth*. But several attempts to create some decent inflation were made in the form of QE. Unfortunately for Japan, QE has simply failed.

The first round of QE in Japan started in March of 2001 under the guidance of the then-governor of the BOJ, Masaru Hayami. And over a two-year period the country increased the amount of monetary supply (by printing money) by over 60%. The end result of pumping 60% more cash into the economy over two years? *Nothing*. Japan's economy was still flatlining, with inflation hovering around 0%. Property prices continued to decline year after year for more than a decade. The continued asset devaluation process was relentless and never-ending. The decrease in the stock market index continued down its ugly path returning to levels not seen since 1982. Yes, the Nikkei 225 index did not fully bottom out until 2002. But talk about a slow bake! That first round of QE for Japan cost $300 billion in printed money. To get no decent result out of such an investment can only be seen as a waste. Clearly in this instance, QE did not work at all for Japan. At best, you would have thought that the BOJ and Japanese government would walk away from printing money ever again. But this shot of morphine (that wasn't really given at a desperate hour to save the livelihood of the economy) was wrongly used. There had already been too many bailouts and capital injections prior to Japan's first round of QE.

Japan's economy fell into recession in early 2001; unlike the collapse of its asset bubble a decade earlier, it wasn't the end of the world. But the team at the BOJ thought that if you pump money into the system to specifically create inflation . . . *it should create inflation*. What they failed to recognize was the scale of the long-term impact of the collapse of the asset bubble. And massive sums of printed money had already been used to bailout and recapitalize certain sectors of the economy, including the banking sector in the 1990s. Because interest rates had been flatlining for the better part of a decade, the Japanese economy had basically become stunted. It couldn't really grow, but it could still take big hits and fall into recession very frequently.

As Japan's economy was taking a beating in 2008 with trade basically coming to a halt, its currency began to build more strength on the back of QE arriving in the United States in 2009. When QE began in America, the U.S. dollar began to depreciate, which was making the Yen much stronger, versus a host of economies whose currencies were pegged to the U.S. dollar. There was also a sharp fall in the cost of a barrel of oil and other natural resources. So as Japan's currency strengthened on the back of weakening oil prices and commodities, Japan's economy was not deflating internally—but the costs of commodities were. You would have thought that Japan wouldn't have been as affected by the GFC if it wasn't for the massive slump in trade. Let's face it, not all aspects of deflation are bad. What would the citizens of a country do overnight if gas became 50% cheaper? *Spend the difference!*

Abenomics

By late December 2012, Japanese Prime Minister Shinzo Abe launched what we now call "Abenomics." This was essentially an incredibly aggressive stimulus plan that added so much liquidity into the market through money printing that there should had been no way that the economy could go down. *As if this hadn't already been tried time and time again on a smaller scale.* But since 2012, more than $2 trillion in BOJ-sponsored printing has entered, and is entering, the economic bloodstream. Is the Japanese Yen becoming weaker? Yes, it is. Great! Now Japan's economy should be able get moving again like it did in the 1980s without toxic sums of debt in the marketplace. Wrong! BOJ Governor Haruhiko Kuroda is overdosing the market with heroin. Haruhiko is doing nothing more than feeding a printing addiction that will not fix Japan's structural problems.

Clearly the Japanese policymakers don't understand that pumping all this money into thin air doesn't work. Like a heroin addict, stock market investors just want more capital gain! And they are certainly profiting from it; but looking at the economic data, we see a completely different tale. The only thing that printing money has done is make particular asset classes become too expensive and overvalued—e.g., the stock market.

Japan has had four recessions since 2008! Between 2008 and the third quarter of 2014, Japan has experienced 13 quarters of economic growth and 13 quarters of negative growth. And this most recent recession has been blamed on the government raising the sales tax from 5% to 8%. Fair excuse! But another lousy attempt at creating inflation! And worst of all, the Japanese government is not living within its means. Clearly, Abenomics will probably not work. When the BOJ has printed close to the equivalent of 40% of GDP in less than 24 months and there is negative growth and recession, whatever the country is trying to do is not working.

This is the classic example of global investors becoming hooked on printed money and those with access to the markets exploiting it, but the remainder of the citizens keep their money away from any opportunity because it looks too good to be true. And I'm guessing it is too good to be true. But this Abenomics story has come out all guns blazing by adding *even more* stimulus in October of 2014: $720 billion worth of printed money. On top of this, Japan's largest pension fund—the government-run GPIF fund—has also pushed its weight into Abenomics by agreeing to buy up more than $1.1 trillion in assets.

Combine the first part of the Abenomics stimulus ($1.4 trillion), the October 2014 addition ($720 billion), and the GPIF investment program ($1.1 trillion), and this is what you have:

$1.4 trillion + $720 billion + $1.1 trillion = The equivalent of 65% of Japan's GDP which will be used to buy up assets and weaken the Yen.

Japan's population is decreasing, deflation is frequent, and growth is simply stagnant. Trillions of dollars have been spent to fight a lost battle. Japan is the world's perfect example of how a country's central bank, politicians, and investors became hooked on QE and are now so dependent on a drug that doesn't heal anything that it will only cost the BOJ more each time it wants to pump money into the system. The sooner the Japanese opt for a new strategy, the sooner this economy will take another big hit and return back to square one. Maybe this time Japan will embrace the evolving demographics and embrace a shrinking population—or open its doors to the world. Either will work.

Abenomics will not.

.

Chapter Six

Europe: The Mess That Was

Over the last 30 years, Europe has experienced quite the economic and geopolitical transition. Twenty-five years ago the Berlin wall fell, creating a reunified Germany. And in the early days of the German reunification process, there were many domestic and social challenges which were incredibly well managed. Look at Germany today. It is united and the citizens are proud to be German. And around the same time, the USSR split apart, and stability finally came to what was once a very divided and tense Europe. Borders around eastern Europe were also being moved, and new countries such as The Czech Republic and Slovakia were being established.

The competitive devaluation of Germany

One of France's most successful entrepreneurs argued (in a private discussion) that the German government worked aggressively in the lead-up to the new millennium and union by reducing the cost of labor. But the Germans didn't reduce wages; they reduced the amount it costs a company to employ somebody. This French entrepreneur said with ultimate conviction that while the Germans were innovatively figuring out ways to allow businesses to reduce their overall labor costs while maintaining wage growth, the French and Italian companies were subject to rising labor costs on top of wage growth. Hence, back in 1999 he knew that inevitably Germany would have ultimate economic power over the rest of Europe. And rightly so—Germany is the best of the larger countries in the Eurozone to do business with, and German companies employ a population that is highly productive and eager to work. As the Germans implemented structural labor reforms in front of the international eye, French and Italian industries became more and more uncompetitive. And throughout the course of the last decade, and up until today, Germany is not only very competitive with its Eurozone rivals, but it is also able to compete for business aggressively with its North American and Asian counterparts. And Germany is probably the only country able to produce an innovation pipeline as good as the Americans. That is, and was, by no means an easy feat. Germany proved over the last 15 years that the value of structural reforms aimed at making a country more competitive can pay off. However, Germany is by no means completely immune to the contagious risk presented by the crumbling economic situation in southern Europe.

Following the modern-day geopolitical transition in Europe, the continent became more economically united. Following the end of the Cold War, it became easier for European politicians from all member states to pull together and integrate the European economy. The idea was that all member states could benefit from the removal of barriers to trade and the flow of money so that the continent's economy would rival that of the United States. And before you knew it, Eurozone member states had a unified currency in 1999 (the Euro) and the key central banking decisions for all member states were being dictated by a unified central bank known as the European Central Bank (ECB). And in and around Europe the British kept the pound and the neutral Swiss kept their franc (although the franc is pegged to the Euro to stop the franc from becoming incredibly overvalued), alongside a handful of other neutral states that were content doing their own thing and remaining independent.

In the lead-up to the GFC, European banks, like the American banks, were highly leveraged institutions that were largely ill-equipped to cover the hemorrhaging losses that were coming on the back of the broken-down IZNOP business model in the United States. And Europe, too, had some credit-fueled property bubbles of their own that had burst, Ireland and Spain coming to mind. In the United Kingdom, London bankers, lawyers, and even taxi drivers were also experiencing new-found super wealth. And with this new wealth, they would go to their banks and obtain big loans to buy their pieces of a very inflated and leveraged London dream. Today the central London property market is mostly a cashed-up foreigners' game; prior to the GFC, however, it was a combination of both cashed-up investors and heavy lending by the banking industry to homebuyers that drove property prices to the soaring heights of 2006 and 2007—before the property bubble went bust.

Prior to the GFC, mortgage lenders in the United States were not alone in lending risky sums of debt to homebuyers. Inevitably, there was a painful reality on the horizon for speculative homebuyers in those European states who thought that their property markets would forever rise in value. In reality, they were living in an unsustainable IZNOP business model that would one day come crashing down.

Ireland

If there was ever a country whose society completely fooled itself into believing that property prices only go up and never crash—and then property prices crashed—it was Ireland. Ireland went into a credit-fueled property bonanza. Ireland, like most Eurozone states, adopted the ECB interest rate and got rid of their own interest rate. This caused the interest rate to drop overnight by close to half.

Construction was everywhere, and property prices between 1996 and 2006 simply shot through the roof. Housing in and around Dublin rose from between 216% to 268%. In Cork, second-hand dwellings rose by an astonishing 316%. This country was simply caught up in the Celtic Tiger mindset that the boom-times were here to stay and if you didn't buy property now, you'd forever be priced out. There were dire warnings from local economic commentators such as David McWilliams and Morgan Kelly, who were desperately trying to warn Irish society for years—but they went largely ignored, and often they were vilified.

At the peak of the Irish construction boom in 2006, there were 90,000 housing starts. Just think about that for a second. A country with a population of just 6.3 million built 90,000 dwellings in just one year. Relative to population size, that's more new housing per capita than even what the Australian's are building today! As Ireland was constructing as fast as it could, there was an influx of immigrants from all over Europe and the world who wanted to get their hands on this new economic dream called the Celtic Tiger. The nation that was once known for mass emigration was now experiencing population growth on a massive scale. In 2007, net immigration in Ireland peaked at 100,000.

The Irish housing bubble went down the same old road as any

property bubble that was being aggressively defended by the powerful politicians and banking pundits. These dominant individuals argued that Ireland was experiencing a chronic housing shortage due to a rapidly rising population and favorable demographics. What these pundits would never argue about prior to the GFC was the amount of debt that Irish households were taking on in order to purchase homes. Of all the IZNOP business models that have been in existence since the Japanese housing crash, this was the worst. The masses were receiving loans at a rate that stimulated artificial demand, creating an aura that there was a housing shortage.

And like in pre-GFC America, as property prices in Ireland were rapidly rising, there were hardly any home loans in arrears. Why? Because property prices were rising so fast that if you had a highly leveraged mortgage and could not pay your debts, you could quickly sell your home, pay back the bank and keep the profit.

For a prolonged period of time in Ireland, it was nearly impossible to default on your mortgage. This was due to the IZNOP business model working its deceiving magic. More money was being loaned to Irish homebuyers year after year, so there were more property buyers in the market all trying to outbid each other, thus raising the prices of property across all of Ireland. Because the default rate on home loans were less than 0.3% prior to 2008, the IZNOP business model completely masked the financial risk that an Irish homebuyer undertook. This shows that when an IZNOP business model is running smoothly year after year, it is hard for a homebuyer to lose or get caught in a sticky financial situation.

Like the American housing bubble, the Irish bubble simply needed a trigger to break down the IZNOP business model. When banks couldn't lend more to homebuyers than they did the year before, all the arguments the Irish politicians, bankers, and pro-property pundits had used as justifications for the rising price of real estate were collapsed. Irish homebuyers were simply overleveraged just like their banks were. Anglo Irish Bank was the bank that had taken the biggest risk, lending to homebuyers via internationally sourced funds through the wholesale lending market. When the global credit crunch occurred, Anglo Irish Bank was the last bank on the face of planet earth that wholesale lenders would want to go anywhere near.

Ireland's economic fate was destined to be added to the exceptionally long list of countries that had attempted to defy the common laws of economics, only to fail. Mortgages that were in arrears swiftly jumped to over 2% in 2009, and by 2011, close to 7% (one in every 14) of all Irish home loans were in arrears. The IZNOP business model was broken, and house prices would to return to their long-term historic ratios; this resulted in an across-the-board 40%+ drop in house prices.

The buildup of government debt

Like Spain (another big housing bubble that went bust), Ireland's government had a relatively low debt profile prior to the GFC. But over the years, Europe as a whole became a swimming pool of government debt.

Government Debt as a % of GDP	2006	2009	2011	2014
Ireland	27.2%	44.5%	87.4%	123.3%
Spain	43%	40.2%	60.1%	92.1%
France	66.4%	68.2%	81.5%	92.2%
Germany	68%	66.8%	80.3%	76.9%
Portugal	62.8%	71.7%	94%	129%

You can see the powerful impact that the European economy had to absorb in the form of governments taking on more debt relative to the sizes of their respected economies just to keep their economies ticking along. So much for governments living within their means!

By 2009, following Lehman's collapse, it was becoming very clear that European nations were taking on extremely large sums of debt. The British government went from having 42.5% government debt to GDP to the 90.6% that it has today. It was becoming all but mathematically unsustainable for a handful of countries to manage government debt without the ECB and Bank of England stepping in and lowering interest rates.

On the back of rising government debt there were large rises in unemployment across the bulk of major European states, with one very notable exception: Germany.

Unemployment Rate (%)	2006	2009	2011	2014
Spain	8.2%	17.7%	21.3%	23.7%
Greece	8.7%	9.5%	24.7%	26.4%
France	7.3%	9.2%	9.2%	10.2%
Ireland	4.4%	12.4%	14.8%	11.1%
Germany	12.2%	8%	5.9%	5%

Since 2006, German unemployment has dropped significantly. The country with all the euros not only rebounded quickly following the immediate impact of the GFC, but it also became the helping hand that would monetarily feed the failing periphery countries.

The PIIGS

Portugal, Ireland, Italy, Greece, and Spain are known as the PIIGS. The PIIGS are the countries that bore the brunt of the economic impact following the GFC. In 2006, Greece already had a government debt equivalent to 100% of its GDP. By 2014, it had shot all the way up to 175%. Italy is one of the largest holders of government debt in the world, and from 2006 to 2014, its government debt-to-GDP ratio rose from 106% to 132.6%.

What a mess! The governments of all the PIIGS were taking on more and more debt to cover the cost of running their governments. As the governments were taking on more debt, their economies were sliding into negative territory. On the back of this, the domestic central banks in these countries were absorbing an enormous amount of assets on their balance sheets to bail out their financial services sectors and other business of national importance. And like the BOJ in its economic downturn in the 1990s, the European Central Bank (ECB) was forced to slash interest rates to stop various governments across Europe from defaulting on their debts. In other words, if you were a retiree dependent on earning interest from money deposited in a bank account, you were inevitably going to lose your income source.

By 2009, Europe had a broad list of serious economic problems, and governments across Europe were being forced both internally, and by their wealthier neighbors, to restructure their debt problems. In other words, they had to solve their financial problems the hard way. This was a lot easier said than done.

Property bubbles had burst, government debts were on the rise relative to GDP, and interest rates were racing south. Both the euro and the British pound weakened against the U.S. dollar from their all-time highs, and the restructuring process began. But the volatility and concern over government debt would not go away.

The ECB

In both the lead-up to and the time following the financial crisis, the ECB was lead by French civil servant Jean-Claude Trichet. He and his team managed the interest rate in the Eurozone and built monetary policy that promoted job growth and economic sustainability. Under Trichet's leadership the euro currency, by all accounts, became simply overvalued. That's a far cry from the early days of the euro. In the early part of the 2000s, the euro declined significantly along with other global currencies against the U.S. dollar. And in 2001, interest rates climbed from less than 3% up to 5% in less than two years. As interest rates rose, the euro began to decline in value. That was definitely not a standard occurrence, but those were the times when the dollar was abnormally strong due to the interest rates in the U.S. rising to stem the tech bubble. And following the post-tech-boom downturn, the euro began a long-term strengthening cycle as the currency jumped from close $0.80c in 2001 to $1.60 in 2008 before the global economy went into meltdown. Simultaneously, the British pound soared from $1.40 to $2.09 over the same period.

This sharp long-term spike in currency appreciation by both the pound and the euro made Europe very uncompetitive in the global marketplace. With Europe becoming a very uncompetitive exporting union, countries like Portugal and Spain became more expensive manufacturing hubs than most parts of America. The high-tech/high-quality exporters from Germany, France, and the United Kingdom were working on exceptionally slim margins. But was this a concern to the European leaders? Unfortunately not. Sarkozy, Merkel, and the rest of the leaders had their egos out of check. They saw the high euro valuation as a symbol of economic strength, when right under their noses there was a banking system that had taken on too much debt and a union that could not export as much as it wanted to because of the high value of the euro.

Like the Fed, the ECB was completely blind to the risks in the financial-services industry. What was clear is that Trichet and his team did not take aggressive measures to stop the housing bubbles in Spain and Ireland from blowing out of proportion in the first place. And, quite frankly, it could have been a case that the property booms in Spain and Ireland were not as relevant in the eyes of the ECB leadership. Like most central banks, they focused on what was happening in the more important north rather than in the south and the far west of Europe.

But as all of the bubbles burst, the ECB was completely caught off guard. Alongside property bubbles, stock markets across Europe were at record highs, peaking in and around the end of 2007. In the latter half of 2008 as hell was breaking loose, interest rates in Europe began to fall. And just like in the U.S., no matter how fast interest rates dropped, there was a world of pain lying in wait for the European Economic Zone. The 2008 downturn exposed a large number of financial challenges in Europe that had previously gone largely ignored. The ECB had no option but to take extraordinary measures to protect Europe as a whole from the internal systemic risks that could have spread from the more exposed nations to the larger more healthier economies.

The PIIGS were essentially economically diseased. And in 2009, it was becoming clear that the risks of contagion needed to be thwarted. While the local central banks across Europe were bailing out their banking systems, Trichet stepped in with a €60 billion bond purchasing program to stem the liquidity trap that the banking system was in. Furthermore, though interest rates were on the way down in Europe, this didn't stop the government bond market from deeming certain countries in Europe as being high risk. The cost for the Greek, Italian, and Spanish governments to borrow was becoming more and more expensive. The ECB purchased billions of euros in sovereign debt from the PIIGS, alongside the commercial bond purchases within the banking system. The European Union was a mess, and Trichet was accumulating assets on the ECB's balance sheet at a rapid rate. By the end of 2011, the Italian banker Mario Draghi took over as the head of the ECB; like his predecessor, he continued to build assets on the ECB's balance sheet.

To put all of this into perspective, in 2008 the ECB had the equivalent of €1.4 trillion of assets on its balance sheet. By 2012, the ECB's balance sheet had €3.1 trillion worth of assets. Talk about monetary expansion! Over that four-year span, the ECB printed at least €1.6 trillion just for "artificial" bailouts! This included a sharp spike in loans to the Eurozone banks. Of the €500 billion in new loans that the ECB made to the Eurozone banking system, the bulk was supposed to be lent to the private sector, but it was collected by the banks and deposited right back into the ECB bank to recoup minimal interest payments. How does the ECB find money to give interest back to the banks that the ECB loaned the money to? By printing more money!

If you've been living in Europe over the past few years, now you know why your bank has so much cash on its balance sheet but so little to lend. The banks feel that it's safer to deposit the money they received from the ECB back into the ECB to make worthless interest than to give loans to small businesses.

With all this cash being printed by the ECB and staying stuck in the ECB, Europe was facing a serious problem: the risk of deflation. On the back of deflation in Europe, you have a stock market that has rebounded from all the free money that has been flying around but has not been in the hands of the citizens. Only the institutional investors managed to get their hands on all of this printed money. So who can blame a European citizen who wants to take advantage of investing in the stock market or bond market, but then walks away from investing in those asset classes altogether? No European with common sense would want to buy into overinflated bonds that offer no return because the central bank is deliberately buying assets at inflated prices with the idea that the problem will be solved by artificially inflating the value of assets—but the same central bank is not willing to invest in, or make banks invest in, the ordinary economy. That was the mess that Europe was in as 2012 turned into 2013. And today, that mess has created a new mess.

Chapter Seven

Europe: The Mess That Is

When you analyze what has transpired in Europe over the last few years, you can't help but become frustrated by how the ECB has reacted throughout the economic crisis. To be quite frank, ECB policy has essentially done nothing to improve the lives of the Eurozone's ordinary citizen.

The winners and the losers

If I was the president of the European Central Bank, and I realized that the Eurozone was in the middle of a credit crunch and that the banking system needed to return to responsibly lending funds to the whole spectrum of the private sector, wouldn't I add a clause in the agreement between the banks and the central bank that the ECB would only loan this money to banks that would loan the money to the private sector after covering the hemorrhaging? The better part of €1 trillion had already been spent by local central banks across Europe to bail out their domestic banking systems, on top of the hundreds of billions loaned out by the ECB. And still Europe couldn't get its act together. Essentially, there's no way that the private sector can ever get a boost from lending if the banks have no money to lend because they've deposited all their cash back into the ECB.

But then again, if a company was a publically listed entity where a lot of the auxiliary printed money ended up, it became more capitalized and it had the ability to access debt. However, since the financial crisis, European companies, like their American counterparts, have been leaning up their balance sheets rather than making them bigger. This means that the prime focus over the last few years for the large publically traded organizations has been to reduce their overall debt burdens. This is in spite of an era wherein interest rates are at record lows and banks are willing to lend as much debt as a publically traded company can take on if its credit rating is good. So the European banking system as a whole is not willing to take on what they would deem to be high risk. Small business owners in Europe will tell you that they've had to live without as much credit as they were used to receiving pre-GFC.

So banks have tightened their lending standards, the ECB has been printing trillions, and a few European states are on the verge of bankruptcy. In the face of this, the ordinary working class Europeans were left to fend for themselves, and, at worst, get taxed more while earning nothing in interest from their life savings. The Greeks, Spaniards, Italians, and Portuguese have taken to the streets time and time again as their governments have tried to reduce costs and raise taxes to help pay for the governments' 1) mismanagement of their own finances, and 2) promises of societal benefits that they cannot afford to deliver. This is essentially Europe's current reality—all because hardly a scratch of the trillions of printed euros ever made it to the real economy. Unemployment has risen in the face of limited returns on investment coupled with little incentive for entrepreneurs to take risk in a continent that has now become addicted to printed money, but has nothing to show for it. Hence, countries like Greece, Spain, and Portugal, alongside Slovakia, are now experiencing deflation. Italy has 0% inflation, alongside the rest of the Eurozone states having inflation of less than 1% (apart from Austria and Luxembourg). So after trillions were printed to feed this economic heroin addiction, the Eurozone is seemingly heading towards deflation.

As Europe appears to be heading towards deflation, so do the returns of the bond market. With the ECB spending hundreds of billions of euros to purchase government bonds, the yields are very low relative to the real risk of lending to countries such as the PIIGS. The German two-year Treasury bond costs money to invest in while offering investors negative returns. The Spanish two-year Treasury bond offers just 0.5% interest. On paper, you would never think that Spain has over 23% unemployment. The artificial contamination of printed money in the bond market has caused a big problem for the Eurozone. Apart from Germany, most Eurozone nations are taking on more public debt than would otherwise be unaffordable to ascertain. Like a housing bubble, investors will jump onto the easy-money bandwagon in higher numbers when interest rates are low. Governments are no different. When interest rates are low, they want to borrow more. The problem in Europe is that economic growth is flat. There is no inflation, which commonly reduces the debt burden. Have we seen this type of problem before? Indeed we have. Japan!

Not learning from the mistakes of other economic failures

When Japan's economy went bust, the BOJ's strategy was to do this:

Absorb a wealth of pain onto its balance sheet and artificially manipulate the market to cater to a very low-interest-rate environment so government debt could be managed while waiting for the economy to inevitably rebound.

But the Japanese economy never rebounded.

The ECB strategy today?

Absorb a wealth of pain onto its balance sheet and artificially manipulate the market to cater to a very low-interest-rate environment so government debt can be managed while waiting for the economy to inevitably rebound.

Unfortunately, copying the same strategy that was attempted by Japan seems to be offering Europe the same fate. So why is Europe doing it? To date, all we see is an overvalued stock market index across all European stock markets and a bond market that hardly offers the citizens any income. And because so many "mom and pop" investors are completely risk adverse in Europe, they're not getting involved in this artificial money maker (and rightly so). Essentially the European main street is not taking risks in the marketplace. The benefit of the main street taking on this strategy is that those who don't invest will not feel the direct impact to the extent that the institutional investors will if the stock or bond markets in Europe collapse. But they will be the end beneficiaries of lackluster growth, recessions, and deflation. This is all because Europe's federalized central bank decided to adopt a strategy that doesn't work. However, there are institutional investors, like in the United States, profiting significantly from stock market investments while being all but assured that the ECB will make concerted attempts to protect these markets from falling too fast. This, in my opinion, is a big bet that can easily go wrong.

What is very clear is that the ECB is attempting to create an incredibly risk-adverse environment so risk can be taken cheaply. Let's not forget that the GFC started in 2008. We are heading towards the seventh anniversary of the demise of Lehman Brothers. Kids who were born in 2008 can now talk, are going to school, and can do simple arithmetic. Time has been ticking along and central banks like the ECB are still trying to solve existing problems. The ECB cannot proactively resolve the problem that Europe's economy has unless all countries start to get their acts together. I'm not talking about only the PIIGS. Because if the status quo continues in Europe, the PIIGS will be known as the PFIIGS.

France

France is the Eurozone's second-largest economy after Germany. It is the third-largest economy in Europe after the United Kingdom. And it is by far the most underrated potential economic hotspot that could trigger Europe's economic demise and close the coffin on a failed monetary union. For years, global focus has been on the PIIGS. But my biggest concern is that the French economy will continue on its downward path to become another "Southern European problem."

As any French citizen will tell you, France has a wealth of structural problems it needs to sort out. And printing money does not solve structural problems. For every €1 of GDP that this $2.8 trillion economy creates, €0.57c goes into the hands of the government and the government can't produce a surplus. It hasn't done so since the 1970s. This country taxes its citizens through the roof with direct and indirect taxes to provide the benefits that its citizens demand. I'm not talking about healthcare, education, and the other great services that the French government provides its people; I'm talking about the generous unemployment benefits and about the fact that the government caves every time when a union takes to the streets to protest. And every time the French government caves in to the protestors, it costs more in tax payers' revenue.

In no country in the world do the employees of a nation complain so much about their employers. If you don't believe me, watch the local evening news if you're ever in France. The first 10 or so minutes of news basically covers which unions or company employees are on strike. And I've seen them all. From the bakers' union throwing flour all over the streets of central Paris while demanding more pay, to the construction workers who believe they should be paid more because their salaries can't keep up with rising costs in a near-deflationary environment! What type of workforce is this? Which multinationals would ever want to set up European operations based in France knowing that it was going to employ people who will view their employers, and the business they work for, as the enemy? In most countries, trade unions are established to provide employees safety in the knowledge that they'll have some sort of moral support and guidance if they're exploited in any matter; French unions look for the smallest excuse to send their union members on the streets to protest. French unions are exceptionally powerful organizations that are dictating how business is done in France. France has one of the highest minimum wages in the world, and on top of this, the working week for an employee is 35 hours. To make matters worse, the French government's backbone has the strength of a chicken wing when it comes to any facet of industrial relations.

France is an extremely socialist country by nature that simply cannot afford to maintain what is a very costly benefits scheme to the unemployed and those in retirement. Now don't get me wrong here. Each country has its own business model, and I respect that. But there are countries in the Nordic region where citizens are getting bang for their buck. Denmark's government collects 57% of all GDP as revenue, and it's clear that the government is investing in its people and their way of life. Denmark is a country that functions. France doesn't function properly. Yet both governments receive the same tax revenues as a percentage of GDP. Like the French, the Danish have a generous social security system that supports the unemployed while they look for work, and the citizens actively seek work. But a significantly larger percentage of the French unemployed population prefer to be unemployed and receive substantial unemployment benefits rather than work. If you talk to business leaders in France, you discover that they are skeptical of all unemployed persons due to a fair percentage of residents who exploit the system and their businesses in order to quickly get fired, return to the unemployment lines, and once again receive benefits from the government.

Youth unemployment in France stands at 24.2%. Furthermore, a lot of these young citizens lack skills. Since France stopped compulsory military service, more youth are spending time loitering the streets rather than learning a trade and gaining the experience that they would have gained in nine months of military service. So as eager as many young French men and woman may be to get into the workforce, it's a case of the chicken and the egg in terms of convincing employers to take on France's youth in what is an expensive country for an enterprise to employ a single individual.

In France there is a population that has essentially lost the drive to excel. France is a country that has achieved so much in modern history—from the Concorde, to the most sophisticated national transport system, to nuclear power. Few countries in this world have the sophisticated level of expertise needed to design and construct extremely challenging infrastructure projects, and the French do it very well! But as other countries are now rivaling France's heavy engineering capabilities, the country can't solely rely on high-end consumer hand bags and designer shoes to take this country into the future. And just as importantly, this country needs to find a way to keep more of its local talent in France.

When I was attending IMD's Executive MBA program in Switzerland in 2013, there were eight French students in my class. Only one of them was living in France, and since graduation, that lone French graduate has since moved to Switzerland. Although just a very small example, this is France's reality today. Highly competent French talent is very much in demand, and they quickly leave France for greener pastures that generally offer more tax-friendly environments on top of the opportunities to rise up the ranks of the businesses they work for.

If France can't retain its talent and entrepreneurs, it will be very difficult for France to ever regain traction as an economy. Let's face it, in America you have the "American dream." It doesn't matter who you are or where you come from, you can be anything you want if you work for it. Today, the French dream is to work for the government in administrative services. Which country seems like it has a future?

If the French government doesn't get its country socially in order and change the mindset of its people alongside workplace reform, this country will become the newest southern European state. And by the way, as long as the French government struggles to live within its means, it is my opinion that France is already a southern European state. This spells disaster for Europe. However, if the French government could start to build a backbone and tackle the lingering issues that have been lasting for decades, the country may be able to structure its socialist profile in a way that makes financial sense. This will not be an easy task, but it is absolutely necessary.

Fundamentally, France needs to find a way to compete more broadly in the global market place. Why Marseille is not as economically important to the Arab world as Miami is to Latin America is beyond me. France and its politicians need to think outside of the box in regards to how the country could create value for international businesses and build its profile as a competitive hub for finance and other industries. I believe that if France fails to reform its economy ASAP, this country will tip Europe over the edge and take down its neighbors. The failure or exit of Greece is one thing—but France is too big to save.

European states have not done enough since the GFC to control government spending. When a high-taxing country like France hasn't produced a government surplus since the 1970s, it's clear that they haven't made serious efforts to contain government spending. Resting on low interest rates to borrow more is what the Japanese government has been doing over the better part of two decades. Has that worked well? No. Will it work well for European states? Of course not. If the ECB prints more money, will it help France to solve its structural problems? No chance!

So as the ECB is providing an "accommodating monetary policy," we must ask ourselves this: Is the ECB's strategy accommodating economic growth? The answer to that question is "No." But is the ECB accommodating the plunge of Eurozone states into more debt? Based on the relevant data points, the answer to that question has to be "Yes." I have never heard of too many real-life situations where those with a debt problem try to borrow their way out of it and actually succeed. In my opinion, this is a case of European bureaucrats doing what they do best—try to solve the problem the easy and popular way instead of pulling up their sleeves and doing the painful work that is required to restructure their country's economy. The economic performance of Europe has been very poor while interest rates have remained at record lows. I firmly believe Europe is attempting to get itself out of a mess using a strategy that doesn't work. Printing money and creating more debt for countries simply doesn't work. History shows that this approach has been tried and tested—and it has failed.

As you can see in the table below, for every €1 of GDP generated in 2008, only €0.987c was generated in 2013.

Year	2009	2010	2011	2012	2013
Eurozone GDP Growth Rate	4.5%	2.0%	1.6%	-0.4%	0.1%

The European economy is still trying to return to pre-crisis levels, but it isn't doing so in great fashion. Trillions of euros worth of bailouts and printed money have definitely not moved Europe's economy into kick-start mode. Far from it! In fact, a broad host of states are driving up the amount of government debt their countries owe by borrowing through artificially low-yielding bonds that are primarily purchased using printed money.

And since most European states already have high taxes, European governments cannot tax their way out of this mess. This just leaves less money to circulate through the real economy. And, like France, most Eurozone states are spending a fortune year after year. Germany, once again, is a notable exception.

Country	Greece	Italy	Spain	Germany	Netherlands
Government Spending as proportion of GDP (2014)	59.2%	50.5%	44.3%	44.3%	49.8%
Government Spending as proportion of GDP (2006)	44.6%	47.9%	38.4%	46.9%	44.8%

While the printing of euros is not going to help the Eurozone recover, neither will government's spending more taxpayer money. But as per the previous table, there is clear evidence that governments across Europe need to change both their revenue structures and spending structures. Italy, Greece, Spain, Portugal, and France can't continue to borrow their ways out of debt problems. These countries must make very concerted efforts to identify where their governments are simply wasting money and where they can improve the taxpayers' bang for their euros. This is a structural problem that lazy bureaucrats create and make no attempts to manage because it's easier to borrow printed money while raising a tax or two, than to problem solve.

If I was a betting man, I would say that each Eurozone country could reduce government expenditure as a proportion of GDP by at least 15%, while maintaining the same level of benefits to their people—they just need to sort through their messes bit by bit and think outside the box a little. If Eurozone governments were better spenders, their citizens would have more euros in their pockets. Europeans would therefore spend a little more and circulate more money within the Eurozone economy by allowing their citizens to feel confident that their governments are spending responsibly.

The ECB has printed enough money to try and test that this was the appropriate strategy. It is not the appropriate strategy. The money printed has never trickled down to the people. And governments have taken the easy way out and loaded their debt profiles with enormous sums of debt. Worst of all, after all this money has been printed to save the Eurozone economy and the banking system, some banks are still vulnerable to collapse because they're still undercapitalized. Twenty-five banks in Europe failed a 2014 stress test; nine of these banks are in the too-big-to-fail PIIGS nation of Italy. You would think that after having printed out more than €1 trillion, the ECB would have already sorted out a bank that needed an extra €1 billion in capital. As you can see, the Europeans are nowhere near solving this problem.

United Kingdom

"This country borrowed its way into trouble. Now we're going to earn our way out." These were U.K. Chancellor George Osborne's words when he presented the 2012 budget in front of his fellow parliamentarians at the House of Commons. This sounds a lot different from the approach taken by many neighboring Eurozone countries, with their preferential strategies of, "This country borrowed its way into trouble. Now we're going to borrow our way out!"

Government Debt as a % of GDP	2006	2009	2011	2014
United Kingdom	42.5%	52.3%	78.4%	90.6%

From the above table, it doesn't look like the U.K. is exactly earning its way out of a debt problem. But on the flipside, when compared to their Eurozone counterparts, the U.K. doesn't seem to be doing as bad in the real economy.

Year	2009	2010	2011	2012	2013
U.K. GDP Growth Rate	-4.3%	1.9%	1.6%	0.7%	1.7%

Although the above numbers don't look so hot, 2014 seems to be looking better for the U.K., with an annual growth rate suggesting growth to be around 2.9-3.1% over 2014. The U.K. economy did experience a double-dip recession with the obvious 2009 fallout before experiencing two quarters of negative growth in the last quarter of 2011 and the first quarter of 2012. But in all, the U.K. economy seems to have some momentum on its side.

Unemployment Rate (%)	2006	2009	2011	2014
United Kingdom	5.5%	8.0%	8.1%	6.0%

In the latter part of 2014, the U.K. unemployment rate was not much higher than it was back in 2006! So why is the U.K. today, at least on paper, doing better than its Eurozone counterparts across the English Channel? Honestly, it's hard to see too much difference. The big difference was the initial morphine shot that was administered early on in the crisis, like it was with the Americans.

The Bank of England (BOE), purchased bonds like other major central banks, and it bailed out the Royal Bank of Scotland and Lloyds Bank. By 2009, it had printed and invested close to £200 billion in bonds and, to a smaller extent, in "high-quality private sector assets." And between 2010 and 2012, it would print and invest another £175 billion.

While the Eurozone has been fighting a lost battle against deflation, the U.K. has done better. In fact, since 2008, the U.K. has had to struggle on two occasions with inflation peaking at slightly over 5% in 2009 and 2011. But since then, inflation has weakened significantly. This period of high inflation occurred when the BOE slashed interest rates in 2008 and 2009, alongside monetary easing and bailouts. The interest rate went from 5.75% all the way down to 0.5% in just a matter of months. And more interestingly, after the second and third round of monetary easing (around the latter part of the second printing money cycle at the end of 2011), inflation was hitting 5% and recession came back to the U.K.; then inflation slowed substantially into 2012. Of course a completely natural economic cycle wasn't in play due to printed £GBP's flying around, but clearly the U.K. economy, in terms of inflation, was more responsive to QE when compared to its Eurozone counterparts. And as the BOE would ease up on monetary policy, U.K. would see slowing economic growth.

The London property bubble

Back in the lead-up towards the GFC, London property prices were skyrocketing on the back of the city's financial-services boom. London is one of the world's two major financial capitals, alongside New York. Even in a normal market environment, London has always been known for having high property prices. Furthermore, the U.K. "resident non-domicile (non-dom)" system has always made London by far one of the most attractive locations for wealthy foreign individuals, who can live in the U.K. without paying tax on their foreign earnings. As long as a wealthy non-dom doesn't repatriate "income" into the U.K., he or she doesn't pay income tax on these earnings. Not a bad deal!

If you know London well, you'll remember that between 2004 and 2007 this city was booming like no other. Money was being thrown around like candy. And bankers, alongside other professionals, were making very big bonuses. There was a mass rush for real estate. And not only were real estate prices rising, so was the £GBP. Renters, too, were paying excessive prices to live in the well-heeled central London neighborhoods. Using the borough of Kensington and Chelsea as an example, in 2004, the median house price was already a staggering 15x household income. That's a big jump from 1999, when the median house price was closer to 11x incomes. But by 2008, the median house price had skyrocketed to 24x the median household income!

That's a high price even for one of the most famous and globally recognized suburbs in the world! Compare this to all the other neighborhoods of London outside the city center—they were also rising at a rapid rate, but were well under 10x incomes. Median house prices across the U.K. over the years have gone up and down like a yo-yo with some well-known boom-bust cycles.

House-Price-to-Household Income Ratio	1985	1989	1997	2003	2008	2009
United Kingdom	3.5x	5x	3.2x	4.4x	5.7x	4.4x

As you can see, the U.K. has taken some big hits to its property market over the last 25 years, as well as having experienced some big rebounds. Today, the median house price in the U.K. is around 4.6x household income. The greater London metropolitan area house price stood at 7.3x incomes in 2013. And since its peak, it's now heading southwards. This is on the back of very strong house price growth in the central neighborhoods, such as Kensington, Chelsea, Mayfair, Knightsbridge, and St John's Wood. Unlike in 2008, this is not a highly leveraged property bubble. It is the result of wealthy foreigners aggressively outbidding each other for premium real estate in one of the world's global hubs.

Here is what has happened to the central London property market over the last several years following the bottoming out of the property market in 2009. London seen the following foreign buyers aggressively looking to buy property:

1. Families and individuals with new found wealth in the emerging world who are looking to buy a piece of real estate in a country and city that is regarded as a safe haven.
2. Wealthy individuals from the PIIGS and other parts of the Eurozone who wanted to shift their wealth outside of their previous places of residence and citizenship.
3. An influx of wealthy Russian, Middle Eastern, and African individuals who were profiting significantly from natural resources and looking to park their money and buy roofs to put over their heads in response to any instability that their home countries may experience in the future.

By 2012 and 2013, close to 75% of all new homes in central London were purchased by foreign property buyers. This is a very large proportion of property buyers in any property market. By an overwhelming margin, the local Brits have been priced out of the central London property market.

Also compared to 2007, the £GBP was much weaker than it was at the peak of the previous property bubble. To put it into perspective, a £1 million apartment in central London at the beginning of 2008 cost around USD$2 million. By May of 2010, a £1 million apartment in central London cost USD$1.44 million. But by June of 2014, a £1 million pad cost USD$1.70 million. As you can see, the London property market is also attractive to foreign buyers when the pound is trading at a weaker rate. As most wealthy foreigners manage their finances in $USD, they see London as a good opportunity when the £GBP is on the weaker side. Furthermore, London's non-dom tax benefit is coupled with no restrictions on foreign ownership of property; there is just a hefty stamp duty on the more expensive purchases. But there is clear evidence that the currency exchange plays an important role these days when it comes to London property. Even the globally rich only have so much money to spend on international property.

Although today's London property bubble isn't fueled by the IZNOP business model, the risks of this property bubble bursting and medians once again returning to 1985 and 1997 levels are very high.

In short, today in Europe, the Eurozone is tethering on deflation, while the U.K. is experiencing some inflation (although falling) and some healthy growth. Another London property bubble primarily fueled by foreign buyers has returned to rear its ugly head—but it isn't credit fueled. The PIIGS countries are still a problem, and France is looking more like a southern European state than a northern European state. The ECB is printing so much money that it has to import ink, and 25 banks are failing stress tests—nine of which are Italian banks. So is the ECB's strategy to print money ever going to work?

Chapter Eight

The Federal Reserve 2008-2014

Like its European and Japanese counterparts, the Fed has been printing money at a rapid rate to apparently cover the shortfalls of what was a painful moment in American economic history. By the end of 2008, it was all but clear that the American economy was going to struggle to stand on its own two feet for an intermediate period of time. In response to America's ailing economic conditions following the collapse of Lehman coupled with a long list of government-backed bailouts, the Fed gave the American economy a shot of morphine to alleviate the pain that the economy was enduring. After throwing hundreds of billions at the financial services sector in 2008, the U.S. economy was still in a shambles following the breakdown of its IZNOP model. Interest rates were sent to near zero. The morphine shot known as QE1 cost the Fed more than $1.7 trillion. Most of this money printed by the Fed was to purchase ($1.25 trillion) mortgage-backed securities. In other words, the Fed was purchasing mortgage securities that had defaulted—one of the crummiest investments a central bank can make. Once you add the $300 billion in treasury bonds and $175 billion in federal agency debt, you understand that this was one very big shot of morphine to ease the pain. QE1 ended in March of 2010.

Following the end of QE1, the United States was ready to stand on its own two feet and heal from the onslaught of what was an astonishing economic storm that hit this exceptionally diverse economy. The initial stimulus package by the Fed did a lot to help the American government absorb a world of pain. And, like many European countries, government debt in America was much lower than it was in 2014. Between 2008 and 2009, American government debt rose from 64.8% of GDP to 76% of GDP. Following the end of QE1, it was becoming more and more clear that the American government would simply not be able to live within its means while it too was absorbing a broken-down IZNOP model. So in November 2010, QE2 was launched. And this second installment of QE would last until June 2011—after $600 billion in treasury notes had been purchased by the Fed.

Government Debt as a % of GDP	2006	2009	2011	2014
USA	63.3%	76%	95.2%	101.5%

Then, 16 months later in September 2012, QE3 was launched. And like a heroin dealer giving the addict more and more heroin, the Fed gave a very big dose of it. Not only did this drug deal of a commitment have no real deadline, it became the better part of an $85-billion-per-month injection into the economy by buying up assets as the American government's debt-to-GDP ratio leveled off.

Housing Foreclosures by Year	2005	2008	2009	2010
USA	532,833	2,330,483	2,824,674	2,871,891

As you can see in the table above, as things began to get worse for America's IZNOP model, the rate of foreclosures shot through the roof. 2008-2011 was a tough time for many Americans. Millions of homes went into foreclosure and the banking system absorbed much of the financial pain from homebuyers who could not pay their mortgages. And then the Fed stepped in and acquired much of these defunct mortgage securities from the banking system.

Many homeowners were forced out of their homes and were told to start new lives with very little but the shirts on their back and the coins in their pockets. The documentaries that show the sheriffs knocking on the doors of homeowners and evicting them make crystal clear how tough these moments were in the lives of millions of Americans, and it was also tough on those sheriffs who were forced to do the dirty work on behalf of the judicial system, the banking system, and the Fed. For years, Americans were told to get into the property market and they did just that. They listened to their political leaders and thought it was okay to take a risk and buy a home through the use of debt—of which there was a chronic oversupply prior to 2006. The IZNOP model was working its magic, and then all of a sudden, 2008 saw it working 100% against America.

So to summarize, the initial shot of morphine (QE1) was supposed buy America enough time to help the country resolve its problems. But when IZNOP business models break down, it becomes clear (like in Japan and many European nations) that the structural problems within a nation become much more evident and prevalent. And in 2008, America was not immune to this. The American government was forced to borrow more money because without the IZNOP model chugging along anymore there would be less income for the government derived from capital gain and income taxes. And in a country that had only once witnessed unemployment rates higher than 10% between the end of World War II and 2008, it was not hard to recognize that all the structural problems would come truly out of the woodwork following the economic fallout of 2008. But then again, the structural problems that came out of the woodwork were, in my opinion, not as bad as they were in Europe or Japan.

Unemployment Rate (October)	2006	2009	2012	2014
USA	4.4%	10.0%	7.9%	5.8%

What I find interesting is the initial impact that the QE1 plus the bailout of the financial system had on the American economy. As QE1 ended in March 2010, the unemployment rate had already leveled off. Having peaked at 10% in October of 2009, the unemployment rate began to fall between the time that QE1 ended and QE2 began in November of 2010.

Unemployment Rate (2010)	April	October	November (Launch QE2)	December
USA	9.9%	9.5%	9.8%	9.4%

And that the Fed launched a second installment of QE was, in my opinion, as if the Fed had delivered an injection comprised half of morphine and half of heroin. Jobs were being created, but the country, more particularly the investors, wanted something more. The expectations were very high considering the economic carnage. Between April and October of 2010, the unemployment rate dropped from 9.9% to 9.5%. Now, under "normal" economic conditions, if a country's unemployment rate dropped by 0.5% over a six-month period, I wouldn't be complaining too much. For example, if the American unemployment rate was sitting at 5.6% and several months later it went down to 5.1%, would you think the economy was going downhill? No. But America wasn't used to such a high unemployment rate, and the effects of the initial shot of morphine were wearing out, so, for one reason or another, American stock investors started to panic. They sold their stocks, and kicked and screamed demanding more drugs. And behold they got their hit! In November 2010, the Fed launched QE2 and bought more securities and long-term treasuries.

GDP Growth Rate 2010	Q1	Q2	Q3	Q4
USA	1.7%	3.9%	2.7%	2.5%

Now, here is my question. In the second and third quarter of 2010, the American economy had what I would call fairly solid growth numbers as compared to the carnage witnessed 15 months earlier. Did America really need QE2?

GDP Growth Rate 2011	Q1	Q2	Q3	Q4
USA	-1.5%	2.9%	0.8%	4.6%

Stocks were falling fast, but GDP was rising! Were the second and third quarters of 2010 the time when the fundamentals of the American economy became less important to investors than whether or not the Fed would print more money? The S&P index rose 4% over the first quarter of 2011 with QE2 in play—even though the American economy was going through a downward cycle in the rebound process. Compare this to a 4.7% decline in the S&P index from the beginning of the second quarter of 2010 to the end of the third quarter of 2010 when America experienced welcomed growth—but without QE. That tells me that there was a very large disconnect between what investors wanted and how the real economy was performing. The Fed printed money, stocks went up. The Fed stopped printing money and stocks went down.

When I look at the eight quarters of economic growth between 2010 and 2011, I'm guessing that this data could be described as a very normal-looking economic recovery with some very good quarters and some not so good quarters of economic growth on the back of the breakdown of an IZNOP business model that rose nowhere near to the crazy heights that it did in Japan, Ireland, or Spain. Believe me, had the median property price in America climbed to 7x household income and then crashed, the situation would've been a whole lot worse for America. But the median house price in the U.S. didn't even reach 5x before its IZNOP business model broke down. So, I'm thinking that because the American credit-fueled housing bubble burst at a lower leverage level as compared to the Irish or Japanese IZNOPs, the overall damage was not as difficult to recover from in the first place. Yes, the banking system had to get bailed out; but, in total, the mess was not that bad relative to scale. America just needed a functioning banking system to get back on track. Nothing more. Now, I know this sounds a bit crazy, but as bad as what happened in America in 2008, there are other countries in this world that, in 2008 and prior, experienced larger deleveraging events. However, just because an IZNOP business model bursts at a lower leverage level relative to household incomes, doesn't mean that the recovery should look like an arrow shooting for the stars. *There are always ups and downs in a recovery.*

Let's use the 1991 U.S. recession as an example.

GDP Growth Rate 1991	Q1	Q2	Q3	Q4
USA	-1.9%	3.1%	1.9%	1.8%

On the back of a recession in early 1991, the American economy rebounded and then slowed down a little. Did the Fed launch a QE program to help the American economy recover in 1991? It did not.

GDP Growth Rate 1992	Q1	Q2	Q3	Q4
USA	4.8%	4.5%	3.9%	4.1%

And by 1992, the American economy was full steam ahead with very solid growth numbers. But, like most recoveries, there are ups and downs.

GDP Growth Rate 1993	Q1	Q2	Q3	Q4
USA	0.8%	2.4%	2.0%	5.4%

And the remnants of the 1991 recession became a thing of the past when the economy returned to its usual up and down cycles. 1993 was a perfect example.

Printing for the wrong reasons.

Since 2010, the Fed may have been overly ambitious when setting high-growth targets while gearing monetary policy too much toward government and stock market fundamentals. It should have been gearing it toward the fundamentals of the American economy—and this error led to printing more money than it needed to. Deep down, Bernanke and his team at the Fed must have been targeting 5%+ growth. A very ambitious growth figure indeed. And, to be quite frank, by 2010, I'm not too sure that the Fed really needed to purchase anymore securities in the marketplace. *The American economy was rebounding*—just perhaps not in the way the Fed wanted. But when an investment community on Wall Street is pressuring the Fed because stocks are falling and warning of dire consequences, this, in my opinion, could do more damage to the American economy than anything else—and, in my opinion, that's what happened in 2010! All institutional investors wanted was a hit of heroin and more capital gain. And by November 2010, they got their injection and Main Street started to fall backwards on the messages of fear that was coming from Wall Street, hence, negative growth in the first quarter of 2011. Should the needs of investors on Wall Street take priority over the needs of Main Street? Well, this is what QE has allowed for. The American Main Street economy (outside the auto sector) essentially picked itself back up off the floor with little help from the Fed.

It was as if key government economists and decision makers forgot that the 2008 fallout occurred because a particular asset class (the housing market) had been fueled by massive sums of debt, got far too overvalued, and then collapsed. And this economic tsunami also took down any asset that was simply deemed overvalued. This is what happened with practically every stock on the stock market. So, why try and get the stock market to rise much faster than the pace of the fundamental recovery story of the American economy? Would the American economy not be growing as fast today if the Dow Jones Index was currently sitting at 9,000 points? Once again, my argument that investors, most particularly retirees, need to earn more income from the investments they make year in and year out to take pressure off government expenditure.

QE2 at the end of the day did practically nothing to boost economic growth. It was the structure of the Main Street American economy that helped America get back on its feet following QE1. But the end result of QE2 was that it hooked an investment community on riding the QE capital gain train. The structure of the Main Street American economy accommodates growth and risk a lot more than the economies of Europe and Japan do. But as witnessed during the late 1980s and the tech boom, stock market bubbles burst when they become too overvalued. The United States still has one of the more competitive tax systems in the west and the $USD is the global reserve currency. America without QE has a lot working for it. But, like Japan and Europe, when you take the interest rate down to next to nothing, retirees who are living off their life savings become more dependent on the U.S. government and its social security and healthcare systems. The Social Security system (SS) in the United States has some very prominent structural flaws. Even former Republican presidential hopeful Rick Perry went as far to call it a PONZI scheme. In essence, it would be an insolvent government entity of the U.S. government if the money collected by SS today was not paying for the immediate welfare of others. And, unfortunately, the American government is forced to borrow to pay for bills and benefits. There is no doubt that the American government must find solutions to the growing costs of SS. In my opinion, it's one of the core fundamental issues that will either make or break America. The U.S. government's expenditure model needs to work fluidly. And there are only a handful of ways to solve such a critical issue. Solving this problem can organically be achieved with low unemployment while retirees have the opportunity to earn more income year in and year out outside of the government pension system. And just as important is that the government avoids approaching the point where it has to shut down like it did in 2013.

Year	2009	2010	2011	2012	2013
U.S. Government Budget Deficit (In $Billions)	$1,413	$1,294	$1,299	$1,100	$680

As you can see in the previous table, the U.S. government has been living well beyond its means in a post-IZNOP era. Big time! But, in saying that, there is a trend that the American government budget could (a very big *could*) end up in surplus by 2017 if it continues to find ways to tighten spending and create more private-sector jobs. In my opinion, the mere fact that a budget surplus *could possibly* become a reality is what separates the United States from France, PIIGS, and Japan. By November 2014, the anticipated budget deficit for the U.S. government was $492 billion. That equates to 2.8% of American GDP. If the American government can produce an economic surplus by the year 2017 and build a government structure that opens the door to several years of uninterrupted surpluses, I think there's a good chance that America may find itself on an altered, yet more prosperous, path than the paths of the PIIGS, France, and Japan. But achieving this requires a great deal of effort. Budget surpluses alongside 3%+ year-after-year growth or higher would really transform America into a fundamentally strong economy, which would leave its main economic competitors in Europe and Japan in the dust. Even a 1%-of-GDP government surplus (used to pay down debt) on top of 3%-annual-GDP growth would make the most astonishing impact. If this were to hypothetically occur from 2015 onwards, this is what U.S. government debt would start to look like as a proportion of American GDP.

Year	2014	2015	2016	2017
Government Debt to GDP	107.1%	102.9%	98.9%	95.1%

And in my opinion, America is in a much better position today to be able to make the transition from budget deficit to surplus. Achieving a government surplus should be America's absolute priority at this point in time. Main Street definitely has its own way of getting itself out of a mess, and it has proven this time and time again. And the U.S. government is not as held back by high unemployment, demographic issues, and an aging population as Europe currently is. While the PIIGS and France are struggling with high unemployment, America isn't; hence, the welfare system has fewer people to look after at this particular point in time, a fact that is making and breaking nations as I write this book.

If Fed Chairwoman Janet Yellen can do anything at this point in time, it would be to pressure the federal government as much as she possibly can to become a surplus government and stop borrowing! And with this surplus, pay down government debt. This is not a Democrat or Republican issue. It's a government expenditure issue. There are enough highly talented Americans out there with the expertise to better improve cost-efficiency processes within the U.S. government to achieve a surplus before 2017. And as unemployment in the United States continues to decline, less pressure is put on the SS system. In this way, Janet Yellen and her team at the Fed can start to progressively raise interest rates so more retirees can one day independently earn an income. However, on the other hand, if government spending in the U.S. cannot be tamed, it too could find itself walking down the same long road Japan has been treading since the breakdown of its IZNOP business model. When it comes to the livelihood of the American economy, what the U.S government does in 2015 will have more of an extraordinary impact on what the American economy will look like down the road. If the government does not proactively improve the way it spends, all bets are off.

Will the end of QE3 mark the end of an era of money printing in America?

In September of 2012, QE3 was launched and the Fed started to buy billions of dollars more in mortgage-backed securities. Why? Well, as former Fed Chairman Ben Bernanke clearly explained, "There's not a specific [growth] number we have in mind. What we've seen in the last six months isn't it." As I have argued in a previous paragraph, the Fed was looking for a growth target placed perhaps much higher than where it should have been targeting. And there is a big difference between Main Street economic growth and printing money that does not end up in the mainstream economy. The Fed is probably going to find that retirees and others who've worked hard all their lives and saved up a lot of cash but are earning no interest won't be the big spenders in the economy that they could be.

In my opinion, QE3 was a heroin shot that should never have been administered. And it would be unwise for the Fed to implement a fourth installment of QE. America is not in the same position as Japan and Europe, nor does it have the same problems. Ending QE would make the $USD stronger and increase the price of American-made exports. But the global growth engine at the moment is America. It may not be booming, but the American economy is by far the best of a bad bunch.

And you just have to look at Japan to get all the confirmations that heroin injections don't work! But America will find itself with the same problems if the Fed continues to print money and inflate the value of assets. America is all about affordable fuel, affordable housing, and an affordable way of life. And in November of 2014, fuel is cheaper, property is affordable across most of the nation, and there are still millions of businesses competing aggressively to win the hearts and minds of the American consumer. This is America's structure. And the country has proved exceptionally resilient through thick and thin within this structure. *Not unaffordable housing, unaffordable stocks, and high fuel costs*. The Fed should have learned from its past mistakes. And I have a hunch that Janet Yellen knows this. But if QE4 becomes a reality, it can be assumed with absolute certainty that it will be just another heroin shot. And it will do nothing to improve an economic structure that, in my opinion, does not need any help. It will just make the end outcome for America worse than what it could be.

Risk of deflation

The U.S. is on a fast road to becoming energy independent. This is an amazing feat and should assure that the price of oil and other energy resources remain affordable. As the price of oil continues to decline, it may be fair to argue that America may not see that much inflation for the next few years *(pending no external geopolitical/trade-related risks)*. And I would argue that if you can save Americans $4 when they fill up their cars, there is a good chance they will go and spend those dollars elsewhere within the domestic economy. That is good news for both consumers and business owners. So, if deflation (very cheap oil) were to arrive at America's doorstep, it may not exactly mean that American households would consume less. With the price of oil and steel coming down in $USD terms, it may mean that more businesses get a bigger slice of the pie. But this in turn may send America into recession. However, as I would argue, that Americans would be spending less by no means suggests that they are consuming less. Americans could, in fact, consume more goods and services, but spend less. These are the trials and tribulations of having a reserve currency.

For example, if the price of oil at gas stations all across America hypothetically fell to $0.50c per gallon for the next 12 months, Americans suddenly would have a lot of extra money in their pockets. While it wouldn't be good for the oil companies, if each American with a car was to save $21 per week on fuel bills and only $15 of that was spent elsewhere in the American economy, the economy would probably fall into recession. But if each car owner on average is hypothetically saving $1092 per year on fuel, is it such a bad thing if $780 of those savings are spent elsewhere in the economy? All of the sudden there could be an additional $115+ billion spent on goods and services other than oil.

If the price of oil continues to decline, it will be very interesting to see in 2015 whether American jobs en masse are either lost or created on the back of oil prices falling.

The Wall Street bubble

I do fear that that stock markets in the U.S., alongside the rest of the world, will deflate. This is a very overvalued asset class and I believe it is a very large asset bubble. The impact of a stock market bubble bursting may not affect Main Street as much as it will Wall Street because Main Street is not a big player in this stock market boom. But we don't have a crystal ball that can tell us whether there will be a knock-on effect that will spill into Main Street from Wall Street when this stock market does begin to really head south.

This time around, Main Street has a lot less to lose. The majority of American households are very risk adverse these days. They have to be when they aren't able to earn a meaningful income stream from the cash they've saved throughout their careers, not to mention the rising costs of university and private healthcare. The U.S. is one of the more expensive countries in the world to get a university education. Since 2003, the sum value of student loans in America has risen by 300%. Healthcare in America, too, is incredibly expensive. These are some of the challenging issues that America faces today. And hopefully one way or another, healthcare and college become more affordable for the American people. It would definitely do wonders for economic growth.

In summary, the Fed has printed trillions to buy up a lot of junk and treasury bills. The value of particular asset classes inflates while we stare down the barrel of Main Street deflation. The economy on Main Street was not a beneficiary of printed money but managed to rebound after the American IZNOP model broke down, thanks to the bailout of its banking system. Job growth is high and the unemployment rate has fallen significantly from its 10% peak. Investors on Wall Street are buying into a very bubbly stock market based on how much money the Fed is printing rather than what the fundamentals of the American economy are telling us. And like Japan and Europe, retirees are earning miniscule dividends on the investments they make in the stock market and cash they have sitting in the bank. But capital gain is what institutional investors are seeking over dividends and yield. And they are hooked on the money-printing drug. Although structural problems exist, America has a much better chance of achieving a government budget surplus in the next few years than its European and Japanese counterparts. But achieving a government surplus requires some highly talented individuals (which America has) to help tighten spending but still allow the government to offer reasonable assistance to Americans in need.

By no means is the American economy completely immune from external economic shocks. But if 2008 was anything to go by, we know that America is still the global safe haven. So, when the wealth of asset bubbles around the world inevitably burst, it is more likely than not that America (and to a lesser extent, Switzerland) will be the landing zone for those who fly to safety. 'Most' American and Swiss banks today (regardless of the help they've had through bailouts) have on paper plenty of liquidity to weather the next economic downturn. However, a compelling case has been made by some well-known economic commentators that the American economy has already cemented its fate as a country in economic ruin. Peter Schiff is a clear example of one who believes this. Furthermore, a fair and valid argument is laid on the risks of the $USD losing its status as the reserve currency, causing the $USD to crumble. The Fed and the American government simply cannot ignore these arguments made by economists such as Peter Schiff and James Rickards. If James Rickards is correct in his forecast, America would have a very serious problem should the rest of the world truly break away from using the $USD as the reserve currency. If this were to happen, my argument that the American economy is the best of a bad bunch could break down. But when I see what is happening in Japan, Europe, and more particularly, the emerging economies of the world, there are much bigger problems out there than the ones in a country that has already seen its IZNOP credit-fueled property bubble burst; a country whose Main Street has gone risk-adverse while the private sector in the emerging world and commodity producing nations are in *risk-on mode with steroids.*

Chapter Nine

Stock Market

Since the global meltdown in 2008, all investment strategies based on fundamentals have literally been thrown out the window. Central banks' strategy of printing money with a proportion of funds ending up in the stock markets has helped fuel a chronic 'heroin' addiction. And since 2009, investors have found success when they've invested into European and American stock markets. And none of these investors have seemed too concerned with earning an income from investing in stocks. It's all been about capital gain!

Barring a handful of asset classes, we're now living in a world where we're surrounded by inflated asset prices. To the everyday, ordinary investor, there is a lot out there that doesn't make much sense—particularly when it comes to investing in the stock market. The table below tells us a great deal.

Stock Index	2007	2009	2011	2014
Japan Nikkei	18,206	7,241	10,882	17,443
U.S. S&P 500	1,563	666	1,361	2,042
Germany DAX	8,034	3,588	7,359	10,030
U.K. FTSE 100	6,730	3,492	6,052	6,813
U.S. Dow Jones	14,166	6,516	12,633	17,626

Clearly Japan, the United States, Germany and the United Kingdom economies are not the powerful growth engines they used to be. Yet, following 2009 when the stock markets in these countries bottomed out, there has been a very strong recovery.

And without having to guesstimate, there's a pretty good chance that the price appreciation of stocks from 2009 to 2014 are not exactly reflecting the core fundamentals of each of the respected economies.

On the one hand, the stock markets in Europe and U.S. look very out of touch with the reality of today's economic fundamentals. On the other hand, there are American and European publically listed entities that are actually performing very well on paper. So, how are these large corporations profiting more than one would ever anticipate in an economic environment that would suggest weak economic and corporate growth? There are some fair justifications that argue that most multinational corporations in Europe and the U.S. have benefited from the China growth story, alongside economic growth in nations that are closely linked to China.

Let's take as an example the Louis Vuitton Moet Hennessy Group, also known as LVMH. In 2010, LVMH made a gross profit of €13 billion, and by 2013 it was making a gross profit of €19 billion. That's close to a 50% increase over four financial years. Not bad at all! LVMH's earnings before interest and taxes (EBIT) have also climbed from €4.3 billion to €6 billion over the same period. This is close to a 40% rise. Furthermore, sales over the same period increased by close to 50% over the same time frame. LVMH's high growth rate is 100% attributed to China's economic growth and the hunger of its nouveau riche to purchase high-end luxury goods. Not only has LVMH expanded its operations in Asia to cater to this new wealth, its existing stores in Europe and America are also absorbing this new clientele base when wealthy Chinese travel to Europe and the U.S. and purchase LVMH products in these markets.

Here is another reason why many publically listed entities are doing much better on paper than what the domestic economies of Europe and America represent. Many publically listed companies have spent the better part of seven years reducing their liability burdens and have leaned up and reduced the risk profiles of their business models and balance sheets. In other words, they've been paying down debt.

Let's take as an example General Electric (GE), one of the world's largest companies. In November 2014 GE had a market capitalization of $265 billion! Between 2011 and 2013, GE focused on leaning up its balance sheet and reducing the risk profile of the organization by paying down debt and other liabilities. In 2011, GE had $601 billion in liabilities. But by 2013, these liabilities had dropped to a total of $525 billion. In just three financial years, GE had reduced in various ways the liabilities it had by 13%. And as sales and profitability remained fairly flat for GE over this period of time, because it holds less risk on its balance sheet, it is viewed as a good long-term investment by institutional investors.

Looking at GE and LVMH, would an aging mom and pop investor looking to receive income each quarter from stock investments want to invest in these two companies, or any other out there at the moment? Here is my take on that question.

In earlier times, we were always told by our grandparents about the 10% rule. Whether investing in the stock market, property, or anything else, you should be looking for a 10% (minus a few costs) return (dividend) in your pocket. GE and LVMH gave investors a dividend/yield of just 3.33% and 2.29% respectively. So, if you were part of an aging couple looking to invest your $500,000 life savings to survive the next 30 years, would getting an annual cash return of $16,650 sound good to you if you invested your $500k in GE? Would an $11,450 annual dividend sound appealing if you invested your life savings into LVMH? One thing is for sure: if you were making these kind of returns over the next 12 months, you and your partner would be earning around what the U.S. government considers to be the poverty line. But what you would be hoping for is long-term growth so that in two or three years from now the dividends would be 20%-30% higher. But still relative to the size of an investment that the non-institutional investor makes today doesn't reflect the fundamentals that would equate to surviving the next 30 years without digging deep into one's life savings.

If GE and LVMH's valuation were offering investors an annual dividend of around 8%-10% on the investment made, would that be more appealing to the mom and pop investor? Absolutely! And should that be more appealing to governments and central banks around the world? Yes, it should. But in reality, it's not what governments and treasuries want, because they're printing money, which inflates particular asset prices, including stocks. And would institutional investors and stock brokers be happy in this type of investment environment? Like governments and central bankers, they would not. Why? Because today investing is all about capital gain.

Artificial insanity

In my opinion, governments and the central banks that are printing money have created a very big asset bubble. With trillions of dollars worth of printed money flying around the northern hemisphere, it is all but 100% guaranteed that printed money has manipulated the stock markets so that they are valued at a much higher premium than what they should be.

Here is another way of putting it. This is the situation in the U.S. as of November 2014:

- Record-low interest rates
- Trillions of dollars printed
- Dow and S&P at record highs
- Corporations that spent close to $600 billion in stock buybacks

Prior to the GFC, investors thought that the good times would never end; then suddenly the Dow index plunged from over 14,000 points in 2007 all the way down to 6,500 points in 2009. Then the easy money in the form of printed money arrived (not that Main Street has seen any of it). So, while the asset bubble was bursting in 2008/09, the Fed gave America a shot of morphine to reduce the overall pain in a moment when the world feared that the world's largest economy was going to fall to its knees.

Fast forward to 2014 and three rounds of QE later, the stock market is offering investors very small dividends. But on the flipside, the stock market offers investors incredible capital gain. Even the publically listed entities think the opportunity is good, and they're profiting in capital gain by buying up their own stock! So the stock market is more focused on capital gain than on providing those who invest in the stock market with food on their plates while they hold on to their investment. In other words, institutional stock market investors are hooked on the heroin supplied by central banks and on making capital gain. How many times over the last several years have you seen weak economic data, but stock prices that are still rising? And to make matters more confusing, when positive economic data did arise, investors would get concerned that the Fed would take away their heroin. Seriously! Who would have thought that the day would come when good news would become bad news and bad news would become good news for stocks? The only way this becomes a reality is when there is an artificial stimulant affecting the value of an asset. Here is an example of the effects of QE. The Fed's first installment of QE was the morphine shot; but when QE2 came to town, you could see the effects of the morphine hit starting to recede, leaving behind a market place that now wanted a heroin hit.

Date	S&P Index
April 2010 End of QE1	1217.28
July 2010	1010.91
November 2010 QE2 Launched	1227.10

In 2010, the annual growth rate in the U.S. wasn't spectacular, but it was positive. But when more and more news suggested that America was slowly finding its way out of the woods, the S&P dropped more than 200 points from peak to bottom. Investors demanded more, as did the American government so that interest rates would remain low and it could pay down government debt. So the Fed caved in and started dealing heroin, and since then investors have been hooked.

It appears that every time the market gets spooked and believes that there will be no more printed money flying around (or as stock brokers call it, "taking away the punchbowl"), investors start to sell stocks. Then the Fed and politicians become nervous, and they continue to feed heroin to investors to stop them from panicking.

On top of all this, the Europeans and the Japanese are also printing money and pumping it into the system. You want to see something crazy? Look at the following table. This just shows how The Bank of Japan—a central bank that has spent the longest time serving fiscal heroin—reacted alongside an investment community when the Fed ended QE3 in October of 2014. Investors became nervous, so the BOJ printed more money, providing financial heroin junkies much relief and capital gain.

Date	Nikkei 225 Index
September 26, 2014	16,401
October 16, 2014	14,366
October 30, 2014	15,783
October 31, 2014 QE on top of QE launched by BOJ	17,048

In a span of 20 days, the Nikkei 225 Index went from 16,401 all the way down to 14,366. That's roughly a 12% drop. What happened following this large drop? The BOJ caved in and announced that on top of the already existing 24-month $1.4 trillion asset purchasing program, they would pump an added $700+ billion into the market. Within hours of this announcement, Japan's largest pension fund (GPIF) also announced it would allocate $1.1 trillion into buying up assets—50% of which to be used to purchase stocks both domestic and foreign. This is a government pension fund managing lifetime savings of many Japanese—and they are definitely not only interested in buying AAA-rated stocks!

What a coincidence that as the Fed closed the book on a third round of QE, the BOJ injected a massive shot of heroin into the investor public on top of the already enormous levels that it had already administered. This stimulus package of printed money sent Japanese stocks to a place they had not seen since 2007. And in less than 24 hours, the Nikkei had soared by close to 1,300 points. Talk about a jump! It was enough to push the Dow Jones and S&P indexes to record highs. Just a few weeks later, on November 17, Japan announced its GDP figures which showed the country was in recession for the umpteenth time in a quarter of a century. When a stock market index such as the Nikkei 225 climbs by more than 1,000 points on a given day, you know with absolutely surety that whatever the economic fundamentals of Japan are at any point in time, there is no fundamental news would ever be good enough to shoot the Nikkei 225 index 1,200+ points higher in a span of 24 hours.

So when the Nikkei 225 starts to fall again after investors become concerned that the BOJ will stop printing more money, what is the BOJ going to do? Print more money? Because $2 trillion+ was not enough? The P/E ratio of the Nikkei 225 is above 20x. This means that stocks in Japan are producing fewer than $0.05c of earnings for every dollar invested today. That's not exactly a stock market where you would go hunting for dividends. And now with the added stimulus set forth by the BOJ, it can safely be assumed that the P/E ratio will only become worse, offering hardly any income to investors. Once again, Japan is in a tough situation; the last thing it needs is to have an overinflated stock market with investors hooked on heroin in pursuit of capital gain.

With 13 of the last 26 quarters of economic growth in Japan being negative, does it seem sensible that the country's stock market index has risen from 7,241 in 2009 to over 17,000 in 2014? Are the future earnings of Japanese publically listed entities going to be able to outperform year after year in a recessionary environment? I don't think so.

The artificial insanity that is QE has really left this world in an abnormal position. With clearly overvalued stock markets in Europe, America, and Japan, how have the central bankers let this problem just slide past them? Is there any historic evidence that what they're doing works? Because all I saw in October 2014 was one central bank (the Fed) walk away from printing money, which was immediately followed by stock markets around the world diving, only to be shot sky high on the back of another central bank (BOJ) pumping in a reckless sum of artificial funds. Japanese citizens need strong dividends to support their retirement, but there is simply no place to find them. In my opinion, this causes Japanese to be more cautious with their money and spend less. Why would a Japanese person invest life savings in the name of capital gain? This was attempted back in the 1980s, and it didn't pan out too well for the mom and pop investors in Japan. Why would they think it would work today?

And unlike mom and pop investors, the GPIF pension fund is going to invest $1.1 trillion of Japanese workers' life savings in a market that attracts minimal dividends. Does this sound unusual? The Nikkei 225 is clearly overvalued through artificial means. The P/E ratio is over 22x. Yet, Japan's largest pension fund thinks it's a good time to invest in the stock market. It sounds to me like a very powerful pension fund manager is under a lot of pressure from the government to take a risk in the stock market that could wipe out generations of wealth. Older people need stable incomes to cover their daily living expenses, not asset appreciation. This stability is impossible to achieve when the value of a stock market is determined by how much money is printed, not by fundamentals.

Europe has the same problem as Japan. Its stocks are too overvalued. The P/E ratio in Europe under the Euro Stoxx index is over 25x. No one is going to find stable income there either! The S&P is offering a more attractive P/E ratio, although, with a P/E ratio of 17x, it is still overvalued. If an investor invested today and in 12 months the stock markets in America, Europe, and Japan retracted on bad news, no matter how big of a heroin shot central bankers gave the markets, one could be looking at very heavy capital losses on top of a downturn, which means that companies would become less profitable and would offer fewer dividends than the measly ones that seem to be on offer by corporations within these three very important economic jurisdictions.

Low interest rates and low returns

With banks across Europe, Japan, and America offering almost nothing in interest, bonds offering nothing, and stock returns not even able to cover electricity bills, there seems to be almost no way to make returns. In fact, over the last few years, the only way to have made money in this economic environment has been capital gain. And we all know that when a particular asset class is a popular investment based on pursuit of capital gain, *it is generally in the midst of a speculative asset price bubble.* Although there are few exceptions to the norm, by all accounts it doesn't matter whether stock markets rise because of high investor activity, QE, a tech boom, or a credit boom—they are all bubbles. And there isn't much that can get in the way of a market that really wants to go down. That is what history tells us. "This time it's different" are the most dangerous words that can be used in economics. And the day the central banks will not be able to offer investors enough heroin to supply the addiction, it will all be over. The markets will want to return to levels that make it attractive for investors to participate based on the core fundamentals. Not based on the drug.

The situation is perhaps the worst for those whose retirement savings are managed by the GPIF in Japan. Is this fund going to be able to withdraw retirees money on their behalves fast enough when this stock market asset bubble bursts? Probably not. Pension funds don't have the best track record of being the first to pull out of a declining asset class. As far as the GPIF is concerned, investors are in it for the long haul! And Japan's biggest cheerleader for taking risk, Prime Minister Shinzo Abe, actually wants pension funds in Japan to make "riskier bets!" How about the funds return better dividends instead??

Greater the risk, greater the reward—or failure. You just need to look at Japan's track record to get a good idea of the direction its stock market, economy, and government debt profile will head when there are no more drugs to ease the pain.

Chapter Ten

What We Know Doesn't Work: Credit-Fueled Property Bubbles

After a review of what the central banks, governments, and investors in America, Europe, and Japan have been doing and how the economies have been performing, we have a much better indication of what seems to work and what doesn't work. And we have to start right from the very beginning again to understand how the United States, Japan, and Europe got themselves into this economic mess in the first place. What we find is that the blame can simply be laid on overleveraged housing markets.

Credit-fueled property bubbles always end in disaster

Since the end of World War II, there have been roughly 40 property bubbles. And apart from all the property bubbles that have been brewing over the last few years, all of them have burst. Since the early 1980s, America, Ireland, Sweden, Finland, the Netherlands, Finland, and Japan, among others, have experienced the wrath of a credit-fueled property bubble bursting—and the effect of that wrath on the domestic economies of those countries was intense.

They all have the exact same ending

When a credit-fueled property bubble bursts, one thing becomes very clear: the domestic banking system will most likely find itself in quite a mess. This happened in every country whose property market and lenders adopted the IZNOP business model. As previously noted, if lenders cannot lend more to homebuyers than they did the previous year in a massively overpriced property market, the IZNOP model breaks down.

As the IZNOP business model develops day by day, the political cheerleaders predictably tell their citizens that a new world has arrived and what is happening in their country is different to any other property market that has boomed only to bust for the last 500 years! All this while the local banking system is pumping more debt year after year into that particular property market at a stifling rate.

My favorite argument is the housing and land shortage argument. While credit is being fueled into the property market by lenders in an IZNOP scenario, society is being told by bankers, politicians, and those with a keen interest in real estate prices rising that there is a shortage of stock. But in reality, there is a chronic oversupply of debt. And society is simply shortsighted enough to believe it! They jump onboard the IZNOP myopia bandwagon. The Average Joe normally thinks that there is no easier way in this world to get rich on paper than to ride the property bandwagon during a price boom. It always amazes me that a property market can suddenly experience a shortage of housing while at the very same time there are massive sums of debt flowing into that particular asset class and construction workers are making up one of the larger percentage chunks of the employed population. When these credit-fueled property bubbles burst, lenders start to bleed money, homebuyers have more debt then they can handle, and construction workers are out of work. Recession hits, and recovery is very painful.

Let's look at California's credit-fueled property bubble bursting. Prior to 2006, there was an apparent shortage of housing stock. Then suddenly construction took a nosedive.

Year	New Housing Starts (California)
2001	149k
2002	168k
2003	196k
2004	213k
2005	209k
2006	164k
2007	113k
2008	65k Ouch!
2009	36k Where's my morphine?

From the peak of the California construction boom in 2005 to the fallout in 2009, there was an 85% drop in new housing starts. What a disaster! Once the American property bubble burst, it hit the American states that had the biggest credit-fueled property bubbles, both in terms of the relative cost of property versus household incomes and in sum value. At the peak of the construction boom, California built a new house (by either knocking down an existing dwelling or building on vacant land) for every 179 Californians in just 2004 alone. Between 2001 and 2006 a home was built for every 31 Californians! Property prices were skyrocketing and banks were facilitating the rising property prices by giving mortgages in the middle of a property market that was mathematically unaffordable to almost all of its citizens. As areas like the greater Los Angeles metropolitan area were experiencing house-price-to-household-income ratios of 10x and 11x and the size of mortgages were rising in sync with house prices, there was mathematically no way to justify how property prices got to where they were in 2006 without risky sums of debt having been pumped into the marketplace for homebuyers.

Los Angeles is the second-largest metropolitan area in the United States, and according to the Brookings Institute, it's the third-largest city in the world by GDP. If you know Los Angeles well enough, you know there are some extreme pockets of core wealth in this city that can only be compared to the likes of New York, London, Hong Kong, and Tokyo. But still, when the credit-fueled property bubble in Southern California burst, the market took a spectacular swan dive.

Like California, the citizens of credit-fueled American states and cities who thought they were living in a property price renaissance were actually experiencing a most lethal business model that has a 100% track record of failure. And like Japan in the late 1980s to early 1990s, that model sucked the life out of the world's largest economy. Ireland and Spain suffered the exact same experience.

Banks fail when the bubble bursts

When the IZNOP model breaks down, banks inevitably fail or have to be bailed out by their government. There is simply too much money lost in a short period of time for all banks who are lending massive sums of debt to households to survive. That's what the math tells us. 2008 was a prime example, when banks across the U.S. and Europe were heavily geared toward the

American, Irish, and Spanish housing bubbles. Once again, driving property prices higher through the use of credit does more harm than any good that is created. And more importantly, we know this IZNOP business model doesn't work in the long run. Eventually, it always breaks down.

Central bankers are always too late to spot trouble

In my opinion, it's inexcusable that a central banker in any country doesn't see a property bubble arising. Furthermore, it's indefensible that nothing be done to get rid of the risks of a credit-fueled property bubble before the situation even gets near that point. There is simply no other asset class in this world that can create so much debt because property is hands down the largest single purchase 99% of people will make in their lives.

Why do property bubbles seem so hard to spot? At least from my point of view, they are very simple to identify when these symptoms arise:

- Property price growth is rising faster than wages and inflation year after year.
- Growth in the sum and percentage of debt borrowed by homebuyers to purchase property is rising faster than wages and inflation year after year.
- Mortgage-debt-to-household-income ratios increase year after year.
- Rental price growth isn't keeping up with house price growth year after year.

These are the four simple ingredients that form a credit-fueled property bubble.

This table below is a clear example of central banks failing to identify when households are taking on significantly more risk than they should be. The data is blatantly signaling the problem. And this is not rocket science:

Household debt-to-income ratio (%)

Country	Pre-Bubble	Bubble Peak
U.S.A	90% (1999)	126% (2006)
Ireland	49% (1995)	173% (2007)
Japan	82% (1982)	131% (1991)

When a society (the citizens) lets greed get in the way of plain logic, and good GDP numbers start filtering through when property prices are rising fast, who wants to spoil the party? Central bankers need really tough backbones to draw a line in the sand and say enough is enough. But almost 100% of the time they are late in taking action through tightening monetary policy (i.e., raising interest rates). There is simply too much historical evidence to suggest otherwise, regardless of country and culture. And unless a central bank takes an aggressive monetary measure early on in the buildup of an IZNOP business model, the IZNOP business model will destroy the economy. Ireland, Japan, California, and Florida had massive credit-fueled property bubbles, and they took extremely hard hits.

Pro-property-price pundits can use any excuse they want to suggest that their credit-fueled property bubble is "different." There is no set timing of how long an IZNOP business model can and can't last, but the longer it wanes on, the more effort a central bank and politicians have made in adjusting legislations to support rising house prices to stop the IZNOP business model from breaking down. That's what happens when the central bankers and politicians get caught up in the bubble themselves. They take all the measures they can to not let the bubble burst. Bad move! This is very evident in several credit-fueled property bubbles that exist today. And there are still countries and property markets out there that still haven't learned anything from the failures of other property markets that adopted the IZNOP business model. In fact, they're taking and implementing incredibly desperate measures to stop their IZNOP business models from bursting.

Why don't the credit rating agencies and international monetary organizations such as the IMF take tougher approaches to the IZNOP business model? From my point of view, no bank that lends toxic sums of debt to homebuyers in the midst of an IZNOP model should have a credit rating of anything more than junk. Remember, IZNOP business models have a 100% failure rate. Back in 2007, what should the credit ratings for Lehman Brothers, Freddie, and Fannie have been 12 months before hell broke loose? They weren't rated as junk. But they were nothing more than junk.

The IMF is the organization that many countries try to woo when they have an economic problem. The job of the IMF should be to stop these credit-fueled property bubbles from arising in the first place. The world spends hundreds of billions of dollars a year on banking and financial services, only to find that 99% of these organizations never spot a credit-fueled property bubble when they're inside the bubble. Without a very powerful neutral voice in the world that has the power to force an economy to wake up to reality, these credit-fueled IZNOP business models will continue to prosper and then crash again and again. And with a global banking system so interconnected, the risk of an IZNOP business model breaking down in one country can easily affect the economy of another country. This is how problematic these credit-fueled property bubbles are. Even a country like Mauritius (which is about as far away from the California property bubble as you can get) went into recession in 2008. This is how globally connected the world is, and the U.S. was the perfect example of how bad things can get globally when an IZNOP business model breaks down.

The IMF is a strong voice in the global economy, but when they do sound alarm bells, they, like central bankers, are usually a bit late to the party. Additionally, they're also ignored by countries when the citizens and political leaders of those countries are caught up in their own bubbles. Once again, it is rather easy to calculate whether a property market is experiencing a credit-fueled property bubble. Are the analysts at the IMF that useless? Is it possible that the voices of the leaders of the IMF are that small?

Stock markets bubbles can burst and not inflict total disaster

As we have seen on multiple occasions in the U.S. since 1987, stock markets experience the occasional collapse. 1987-88 was the occasion of one, as was the tech boom era. Then we had 2008. America fell into recession in the early 1990s and in 2001, but these two downturns were nothing like that of 2008. Why? Because there was no overly inflated IZNOP model to burst. Although property prices were creeping up by 2001, they were nowhere near the heights they reached in 2006. But had the IZNOP model burst in 2001, it would have been a very early burst in the life of a credit-fueled property bubble, thus it would have caused significantly less pain than it did in 2008.

In Japan and Ireland, too, the impact of a credit-fueled property bubble bursting is far worse than any stock market crash that happens without a credit-fueled property bubble bursting. That is what history tells us. Just think about it. As with 2009, did the Fed have to take the same monetary measures in the early 1990s or in 2001 when those recessions hit? No. Did the Fed introduce three rounds of QE? No. Did interest rates fall to near zero and permanently flatline in either of those downturns? No. But when the property bubble burst, all hell broke loose, and America appeared to be on the exact road that Japan took in the early 1990s.

The biggest economic disasters always include a credit-fueled property bubble. As long as central bankers around the world don't make the effort to make an early diagnosis based on four very simple data points, we are all but guaranteed to see more IZNOP business models break down and cause economic havoc. And there are credit-fueled property bubbles in existence today that will leave you bewildered when you benchmark them against America in 2006.

Chapter Eleven

What We Know Doesn't Work: Countries Loading Up On Government Debt and Old People

In recent years, it has become more and more clear that many European governments will become more dependent on borrowing to keep their social system's functioning. This is what Japan has done for a long time. And from the looks of it, countries like France and Italy are going to try to take the easy way out of this problem only to leave future generations of their citizens to pay the debt.

We know that as populations get older and more people enter retirement while fewer people enter the workforce, an economy will generally have less economic productivity. Meanwhile, the cost for government to maintain benefits increases in sum. In other words, the result is a situation wherein the government can only increase expenditure by raising taxes and borrowing more. The alternative option is to take a no-nonsense approach and build an economic model around tighter government spending, as well as make it possible for younger generations to keep more of the money they earn so they can spend it in the domestic economy. But for some reason, Japan, alongside some of the broken southern nations in Europe, has difficulty doing this. And this is impossible to do in a zero-interest-rate environment, because:

No Interest = More Government Liabilities

Japan, for example, is caught in a lose-lose situation. Their middle-class retirees have very little access to financial products that offer a reasonable dividend to live off. Furthermore, the BOJ is keeping interest rates at zero so the government can borrow more year after year to cover costs and benefits. If Japan didn't have a credit-fueled property bubble in the first place, it would be all but guaranteed that the interest rate today in Japan would be a lot higher than zero. It would also be a given that government debt would be nowhere near as high as it is today. This would mean that Japan would not be living as far beyond its means as it is today. Let's face it—which of the two hypothetical retirees is more of an economic liability to a government:

- A retiree with $400,000 in savings earning 6% interest at the bank?
- A retiree with $400,000 in savings earning 0% interest at the bank?

The retiree with $24,000 in income from savings has a much better chance of not requiring government benefits than the retiree who is earning nothing but is eating away at his or her life savings day after day to cover the cost of living. On top of that, the retiree with income would be paying a little bit of income tax alongside his or her greater purchasing power. But in Japan, the interest rate is zero, so there is no income for anyone who keeps money sitting in a bank. I cannot emphasize the damaging impact a zero-interest-rate environment has on a government budget. Today in Japan, you have close to 25% of the population in retirement. That's a large number of people who need to be looked after if they're not earning any dividends or interest to cover daily costs. Furthermore, the average Japanese retiree will live a very long life. And the children of these retirees, who are of working age and are earning middle-class wages, cannot afford to look after their parents and start families of their own at the same time.

To clarify, the old-age pension in Japan is roughly $7,000 per year. In some parts of Japan it would be very hard to survive off of this sum of money. If the banks in Japan were offering deposit holders 6% interest, a retiree would need to have saved $118,000 over his or her career to receive the same income as the pension. What would the difference be? If the retiree was off the pension and living off interest from deposits in the bank, the Japanese government would save $7,000 a year. Multiply that by however many Japanese live off the government pension, and there is the possibility for substantial savings. For example, let's assume 25% of all retirees on the government pension have on average $120,000 in cash in their life savings that earns no interest. If they *were* earning 6% interest on their life savings and were taken off the pension, the government would save $55 billion a year in pension payouts with no decrease in money coming in for the retiree. Furthermore, Japanese retirees who have significantly more retirement funds (for example, $1 million in bank deposits) would be earning $60,000 a year in interest, which would be both taxable income and more purchasing power than the zero interest the retiree would be earning today. That would be a win-win for both the government and the domestic economy as Japan's population declines.

But what we know is that Japan, like a handful of European countries who aren't far behind Japan in terms of demographics, is living in a zero-interest-rate environment, and the cost to acquire assets are very high relative to the possible dividends that can be earned. The big problem here is that when a government is too focused on spending and taxing rather than generating purchasing power for its retirees, a country is destined to economically struggle for an infinitive period of time. Once again, Japan is a very clear example of what doesn't work.

When making a promise to the public that they will have a pension in 40 years' time

Nobody has a crystal ball. It's practically impossible to predict what the global economy will look like in 40 years. But back in 1971, social European governments like France and Italy were promising their populations that the taxes they paid then would cover their retirement costs today. Have the taxes that the newly retired Frenchman paid over the last 45 years been sitting in a government bank account accumulating interest? No. Those taxes have gone into social services and into the pockets of the generation of retirees and unemployed before his retirement. Furthermore, because his government hasn't been able to produce a budget surplus since his first day at work back in 1971, the French government has had to borrow money to help pay for his social benefits. But the French government made a promise and said he would be secure in his retirement because he paid taxes. And the French government back in 1971 assumed that this French citizen, alongside every other French citizen who started to work in 1974, would on average only live to see the age of 75 years old, leaving only a handful of years for the retiree to be on the pension. But today in France, the average woman and man will enjoy 27.4 and 22.6 years of retirement respectively. That is a lot of pension money for the French government to pay over that period of time.

Today, France already has over 11.2 million citizens over the age of 55. And by global standards, France has a low labor force participation rate, a high unemployment rate of over 10%, and 92% government debt to GDP. What a mess!

Labor Force participation rate (%) 2012

Country	
Japan	59%
France	56%
Italy	49%
Greece	53%
Spain	59%
U.S.A	63%
United Kingdom	62%
United Arab Emirates	79%
Germany	60%

It's funny how the countries with the more socialist economic systems have the lower labor-force participation rates. There are a lot of French and Italians of working age who are simply not participating in the workforce.

But while you have the extremely socialist leader Francois Hollande running the show in France, you know he is battling for French socialism—*the unaffordable socialism.* In September of 2014, Hollande had an approval rating of just 13%. And I think it has become pretty clear that the French population (who voted him into the presidency in 2012) are now starting to realize that the French system is breaking down. France is simply not able to live within its means, even though the nation taxes every facet of its citizens' lives. Inevitably, France—like Italy, Greece, and other nations in Europe overwhelmed by their generous social security benefits—will have to take another approach to the status quo.

Europe can learn a lot from Japan, because we know that what Japan has attempted to do doesn't work. An aging population coupled with 50% of GDP in government expenditure is simply too much for a country to handle in the midst of a zero-interest-rate environment that has few investment products offering meaningful dividends.

We know that Japan's retiree model doesn't work. France's current retiree model doesn't work. They are both too expensive for the rest of the economy to cover the shortfall. Furthermore, as the population of retirees grows in a zero-interest-rate environment, more will be forced onto the government pensions as their life savings are spent quicker than they would be in a higher-interest-rate/dividend environment. It is simply not sustainable. And as you will see in the recommendations chapters, it will be inevitable that many central banks and politicians will need to take alternative measures to compensate for an aging population.

Government debt

On top of the demographic challenges that many of the world's economies will face, government debt is increasing around the world at a stifling rate in an economic environment that lacks inflationary pressure. I don't think that government leaders and their central banks see government debt as a serious problem, but rather they see it as a solution—without figuring out how to pay back the debt. On one side of this argument, it is fair to say that government debt didn't cause the collapse of the Japanese economy in the early 1990s. Neither was it the trigger that caused the GFC. But it is the one very issue that is holding central banks back from raising interest rates today. This is because when an economy nose dives, a government will generally absorb a lot of pain. This is handy to have in the midst of an economic meltdown. But if a country cannot financially stand on its own two feet by means of government expenditure, borrowing year after year eventually starts to take its toll. More particularly when the funds are borrowed to pay fixed costs such as social security rather than investing in *meaningful* infrastructure that is actually going to be used and will boost GDP growth over the long-term. Building a new freeway that cuts travel time by 30%, or constructing a new airport that's going to be able to handle more passengers and airlines—that's how governments should be using debt to pump into their economy. Not social security. Essentially, whatever government debt is used for, that investment should be able to pay for itself through either of the following:

- o Meaningful economic purposes
- o Taking in fees
- o Reducing workable hours wasted (saving time)

- Improving health of the population

So even though it was not high government debt that triggered recent economic storms, today it is the catalyst of the problem many countries face. Once again, it's very hard for Japanese retirees to financially stand on their own two feet over the lives of their retirements if they're grinding away at their life savings instead of being in the situation where their life savings generate meaningful income. Zero interest rates, measly dividends, and gross rental yields for property investors are too low to generate decent incomes in Japan. What if the cost of Japan's assets were half of what they are today? Japanese investors would be getting twice the returns. It's as simple as that. But while Japan's government and its central bank are collaborating to increase government debt levels, they are essentially not allowing its people to hunt for yield because there is none!

The dividend crunch

-Nikkei 225 index valuation close to 25x earnings
-Zero interest
-2%-3% net yields on property investments

As the BOJ helps the Japanese government consistently live beyond its means, there occurs what can be called a dividend crunch. Unless the BOJ and the Japanese government take on a serious structural reform strategy, this dividend crunch will slowly eat away at the life savings of its retirees and keep more Japanese on the government pension. When it comes to printing money and government debt, it is, in my opinion, the lesser of two evils to pay down (in very small increments) government debt with printed money than to buy up more debt in a deflationary environment. But this simply cannot be achieved unless the Japanese government first starts to live within its means. This means restructuring the country's economic model to adapt to the changing times.

European countries are only a few years behind Japan with the same serious problem. And the ECB is taking a strategy that allows government access to cheap debt when it should be pushing countries to pay down debt, not borrow more! And, yes, this may include a period of deflation. But, in my opinion, deflation may not be a bad thing for citizens at this point in time!

To better illustrate the problem at hand for Japan and Europe, let's look at two hypothetical countries that we'll call Country A and Country B.

Retiree Financial Portfolio $400k cash/$100k stocks	Country A	Country B
Life Savings	$500,000	$500,000
Annual cost of living	$30,000	$30,000
Interest rate at bank	7%	0%
Annual stock dividends	7%	2%
Annual income from interest	$28,000	$0
Annual income from dividends	$7,000	$2,000
Total Annual Income	$35,000	$2,000

Let's say that the government of Country A lives well within its means with a government debt-to-GDP ratio of just 12%, as compared to Country B's 120%. Both countries have a national sales tax of 5%, and $500,000 is what the average retiree will have in cash and stocks on the day of retirement. As with most countries, there are retirees in Country A who simply do not retire with this amount of funds to their names. Although Country A's government has a government pension plan of $350 a week, it's not widely utilized by its retirees, due to the fact that the life savings of the vast majority of the retired population offers a better income than the pension. Also like most countries, 15% of the retirees had very long stints of unemployment throughout their careers and had no way to save such an amount of money; these are the people who ended up on the pension plan.

Because Country A has a very low government debt profile to pay off, and year after year it produces either a small budget surplus or break-even expenditure, the government doesn't have to repay much debt each month. Even though the government borrows money at 8%, it is living well within its means. Country A also has a retirement system that forces employees to save throughout their career. Of what they earn in income, 8% must be kept in cash, plus another 2% can be invested elsewhere in asset classes such as the stock market or other various funds. This cash is locked away in a bank account at one of the country's government-owned financial institutions earning 7%

interest over the course of the employee's career. So when the employee starts his retirement, he has $500,000 in capital to earn him an income.

Furthermore, because the central bank in Country A maintains a high interest rate at around 7% to meticulously stave off inflation, the costs of acquiring assets are always affordable. *This means that the private sector too has a very low level of leverage relative to GDP.* Because assets across the board, including housing, are very affordable, not much debt is required to purchase a home. And the banks in Country A don't have to venture overseas to find more funding. This central bank doesn't like it one bit when its property market makes the slightest attempt to rise faster than incomes, and it acts very swiftly to raise rates when this occurs and sends a strong message: "Don't overpay for property!"

Because the mass bulk of private sector debt in Country A is derived from domestic bank deposits, the banking system is very conservative when it comes to lending to both homebuyers and businesses. Also, interest rates for mortgage holders are always hanging around the 10% range. Once again, Country A doesn't like expensive assets. But what Country A does like is that even though its aging citizens aren't working anymore, they're earning income from banks that are lending very responsibly and conservatively to homebuyers and businesses. Furthermore, as Country A likes to keep up with the times, it invests heavily in *meaningful* infrastructure to help improve the lives of its citizens and boost economic growth.

Despite an aging population, Country A is able to live well within its means because the average person generally retires with $400,000 in cash and $100,000 in stock to live off. Both cash and stocks offer a net return of 7% in the retiree's pocket. So, the average retiree is earning enough income to live a comfortable retirement and doesn't need to live off the government pension plan, and, therefore, is not a financial liability to the government, but an asset. The $35,000 a year in interest and dividends that the retiree makes is generally taxed at 10% on his annual earnings that bear no deductions. So the government of Country A will not only make $3,500 in income tax revenues, but it will also make an extra $1,500 per year revenues through the 5% sales tax, as it costs $30,000 a year to maintain a great quality of life—which the retiree will use his or her own purchasing power to pay for.

In addition, because the debt profile of the publically listed corporations in Country A is extremely low, these entities themselves are also living within their means and don't carry the high risks associated with excessive leverage. And as these companies offer investors a 7% dividend and even better P/E ratios, they are a fantastic investment.

Meanwhile, Country B's government is trying to figure out ways to cover its costs. It does this through the assistance of its central bank printing money and buying up government debt so Country B can make its welfare payments. Like Country A, Country B has a fast-growing population of retirees. But because the government has a high debt profile, in order to make the government's interest payments at an affordable 1.2%, the central bank keeps interest rates at 0%. So while Country B is experiencing a low-interest-rate environment (on top of a stock market that's rising because of all this money printing), the average new retiree has a problem: the $500,000 in cash and stocks he owns are earning a net return of $2,000 a year. And because the retiree is not a speculator, he is not consistently buying and selling stocks and making capital gain.

So, after five years of retirement, the retiree has earned a grand total of $10,000. Because it costs $30,000 to live each year, this retiree has burned through $140,000 in cash after five years, leaving him with just $260,000. So the retiree is forced to go on the government pension. And let's say the pension is $350 per week, or $18,200 a year. It costs this retiree $30,000 a year to live a comfortable life in retirement. But because the retiree now has this pension of $18,200 a year coming in, he realizes that he must be able to live off this pension or he will have no cash and stocks to leave for his children when he passes. So he tightens the belt and reduces both his living conditions and his quality of life. With $18,200 a year from the government plus $8,000 a year from his life savings, the retiree now has $3,800 a year less to live off. That equates to fewer lunches out with friends, smaller Christmas gifts for the grandchildren, no holidays, and overall less consumption—all while being a heavy cost to the government.

So this retiree is now a liability on Country B's balance sheet. This retiree could've easily lived within his or her own means if Country B had a banking system that could provide a fair interest rate relative to the risk the bank was taking with the money deposited. On top of this, if the stock market wasn't so overinflated because of all this money printing by Country B's central bank, the retiree would've been earning a better dividend that would've justified the risk taken in a high-risk economic environment that offers no yield!

Because there are so many retirees living off the government pension in Country B and retirees make up such a large proportion of the population, the government has to spend a lot more on pension checks than Country A does on its retired population.

Retired Population	Country A	Country B
Population in retirement (%)	25%	25%
Proportion of retirees on the government pension (%)	15%	70%

As you can clearly see, 70% of Country B's retirees are on the pension. This equates to 17.5% of the entire population. As for Country A, 15% of retirees are on the pension. This equates to just 3.75% of its population. Once again, which government has fewer overheads here? Which country is likely to deliver a budget deficit?

Countries like France are looking like they will end up with the same problems as the hypothetical Country B. Such a large proportion of the retired population is one day going to take on the pension, that it will be all but impossible for the French government to pay its bills without taking on more debt. And because government debt in France is already nearing 100% of GDP, the government wants a low interest rate, while the retirees want a higher interest rate and dividend so they can live within their means and not become dependent on a government pension plan that may one day force the French government to reduce the pension offered to retirees. This is the high price paid by a country that takes on too much government debt and fails to assess how much it will cost to pay the pension for millions of citizens when many could have possibly managed to live within their own means if they were making interest and dividends from their life savings. This is not just a problem for France and the PIIGS; this problem applies to any country with a welfare system that is year in and year out unaffordable due to high government debt, printed money, no interest rate, and overinflated assets that give measly dividends.

This is what is happening in Japan today! Following its economic downturn in the early 1990s, this country should have been fighting tooth and nail to make all asset classes affordable so that every retiree could earn livable income from their retirement savings—but Japan took the complete opposite approach. And furthermore, a huge chunk of its aging population was overloaded with toxic debt from the lending binge of the 1980s. And look at Japan today! It is still one big mess! Japan's government wouldn't have had these costs to cover in the first place had the BOJ kept interest rates higher with assets prices that provided a livable return on income.

In some countries, like Australia, the government already forecasted back in the 1990s that structural reform was required so that one day people would be able to stand on their own two feet when they retired. This should one day reduce the government cost of having an aging population. And as long as Australian retirees and the funds that manage their life savings don't take their retirement packages and return to the bank for highly leveraged loans to buy overly inflated and highly leveraged asset classes in an IZNOP model, you would think that as long as Australia offers an interest rate above 7% that the vast majority of retirees will be able to live within their means. So with Australian government debt to GDP at 21%, you'd think that this country would have its act together. But just because you have low government debt and banks offering some interest to deposit holders, *doesn't mean all the bases have been covered*. In 2007, Ireland had a government debt-to-GDP ratio of just 24%.

We have a very clear indication of business models that do not work—you'd think that governments and central bankers would have learned a thing or two about economics. Credit-fueled property bubbles always burst, leaving in ruins countries that thought "this time it's different." This type of asset bubble is also the trigger that opens a can of worms in the form of government debt and an interest rate environment that leaves a population of retirees unable to live within their own means—which creates more costs than a government should outlay to cover the living expenses of a growing proportion of a population. Once households that took on excessive debt get burned, the responsible citizens who saved cash would get burned in the form of no yield. So did central bankers from around the world learn from this valuable lesson? I think we can all agree that the answer to that question is a resounding "no." And there is no better example of this than a country that could one day make what happened in the United States, Europe, and Japan look like a walk in the park.

Chapter Twelve

China

There are asset bubbles . . . and then . . . there's China

In my previous book, *Australia: Boom to Bust*, I argue that China is the economic "bubble to end all bubbles." And, in my opinion, for a very good reason. There has been no other country over the last 20 years—quite possibly throughout human history—that has transformed so quickly in such a short period of time. Not one!

We could never argue against a government and a central bank's willingness and desire to pull its population out of poverty and give its citizens a better way of life. But we can argue about whether a particular nation is adopting the right strategy while doing so. It's important to ask ourselves if the strategy that China is taking is sustainable. To date, and at face value, you would think China has been the miracle global economy that is successfully pulling its people out of poverty at a relatively fast rate. However, history has a good track record of repeating itself, therefore, it's quite clear how China's thirst for rapid growth will eventually backfire. Although we're told that China is different and that this is their century, I fear that the world has underestimated the sheer scale of risk taken to get this economy to the heights it has reached in such a short period of time.

GDP (In Trillions)	1999	2003	2007	2011	2013
China	$1.083	$1.640	$3.495	$7.324	$9.184
USA	$12.32	$13.53	$14.99	$15.19	$15.92

In $USD terms, between 1999 and 2013, the Chinese economy grew by 848%. Think about that for a second. Over the same period of time, the American economy has grown by just over 22%. Does this level of hyper-growth in China seem sustainable to you? If China's economy grows by the same rate over the next 14 years from 2013, it will become a $77 trillion economy by 2027. Now that is highly unlikely to happen. But in saying that, we need to understand how China went from a $1 trillion economy to a $9 trillion economy in a span of less than 15 years.

Now, if you've ever been to China or you're a regular business traveler to China, you can't help but be truly amazed over how this country has physically transformed. This transformation, in my opinion, was no easy feat. No country in the world has built new infrastructure and housing at such a scale—so much so that roughly 46% of China's GDP is geared toward fixed asset investment. We must ask ourselves whether all this investment into housing and infrastructure is for *meaningful* economic purposes or is it just to stimulate GDP. Because this country is constructing like there's no tomorrow.

Fixed Asset investment (2012)	Proportion of GDP
China	46.1%
United Kingdom	14.2%
Japan	21.2%
India	29.9%
European Union	17.8%
United States	12.8%
Australia	28.5%

Relative to scale, China is the world's third-largest annual investor into fixed asset investments as a proportion of GDP. Only the Republic of the Congo and São Tomé and Príncipe spend a greater proportion of their GDPs on fixed asset investments. So when the world's most populous country (more than 1.2 billion people) spends a massive amount of its GDP on construction, they must be building an astronomical amount on infrastructure and housing. This requires a lot of steel and other raw materials, such as cement.

Cement Usage	Cement Consumption
USA (1901-2000) or 100 years	4.5 Gigatons
China (2011-2013) or 3 years.	6.6 Gigatons

The above table tells you how much China must be constructing year after year. Mind-blowing. America, hands-down, is the world's largest economy that has transformed significantly while reinventing itself time and time again. In the twentieth century, America (even with only roughly 23% of China's population) built housing for all its citizens and infrastructure at a massive scale over and over again. But still, between 2011 and 2013 alone, China consumed 32% more cement *in three years* than the United States did *in all of the last century*. This is hands down the best way to describe the massive scale of this construction binge in China.

As Europe, America, and Japan have spent the better part of the last six years licking their economic wounds, China has continued to accelerate. At a desperate moment in 2008, China made a $500 billion+ stimulus package that was focused on growing the scale of its construction activities. New cities are being constructed all over the country, and property investors have been rushing to get their hands on any piece of real estate they can. Furthermore, some of the most globally recognized household names in the high-end luxury consumer industry are vying for the best store locations in major Chinese cities to offload expensive inventory to a new client demographic that didn't exist just a decade ago. But for one reason or another, it's seems as if nobody has used a calculator to properly forecast how much infrastructure this country will actually need for its population.

Meaningful infrastructure

I fear that China has built an economy that has core fundamentals that make absolutely no sense. This is what happens when a country is focused purely on the GDP growth number rather than on *the meaningful quality* of the GDP growth that is created. Let's face it, it's no secret that China has built a slew of new cities that are called ghost towns. These ghost towns are new cities that have been built literally from scratch and today stand relatively empty compared to the scale of infrastructure built in and around them. "Build and they will come" has thus far been the strategy in China.

Many of these new cities have it all, everything from new underground metro-rail systems to new airports to new stadiums. However, what many of these new cities lack is people. There are simply not enough people moving to the new cities that have been built. So, on one hand, it's not as if all the local Chinese governments combined haven't built enough new cities to be able to cater to the greatest human migration of all time. But these local governments are competing against each other for people to move to their locales versus other local jurisdictions. Local Chinese governments have definitely made genuine attempts to provide all of the necessary First World infrastructure, and they've leveraged their local governments through the roof to do so. In saying that, these municipalities all across China are competing very aggressively to win the hearts of business owners and a new urban population. And each local government in China is competing to have the highest economic growth rates in the nation. And I am not talking about the major well-known and established Chinese business hubs like Shanghai, Beijing, or Guangzhou; I'm describing the hundreds of second-, third-, fourth- and fifth-tier cities unknown to almost anyone outside of China. They are unknown, but they're all building infrastructure and housing at a rapid rate.

As China's central government wants to have more than 70% of its population urbanized by 2030, it's becoming quite clear that every local government thinks that its region will be a major beneficiary of one of the greatest human migrations of all time. It is anticipated that 233 million Chinese will move from the farms to the cities. However, there are simply hundreds of new cities coming out of the woodwork, and what is becoming very clear is that many local governments will never be successful in their bids to attract new domestic migrants to their locales. The world's most populous country already has an oversupply of cities. So the big risk is that there's all of this new world-class infrastructure that may never be used in the bulk of new cities that are being created out of thin air. While the local governments that manage all these new cities are waiting—and praying—for new residents to move into their new cities, there are a wealth of bills to pay and debts to cover.

China's development strategy of *build and they will come* is generally an unusual one to take, because it financially requires so much initial outlay and debt. Each local government is competing for private sector business so hard that they've taken enormous financial risks in terms of borrowing to build. Local government debt in China grew from 15% of GDP in 2005 to roughly the equivalent of 44% of GDP in 2013—that is equivalent to 1020% (10.2x) in sum-growth in local government debt in just eight years. Pretty crazy when you think about it that way, considering total inflation over the same period rose by just 24%! For $1 in local government debt in 2005, today there is $10.20. And by all mathematical accounts, it will never be repaid. What has practically all of this debt been used for? Building housing and infrastructure—*much of which may never be meaningfully utilized.*

Housing

In the first 11 months of 2013 alone, China was constructing 6.460 billion square meters of real estate, 4.729 billion of which was residential real estate. To put that into perspective: for every Chinese resident, 3.45 square meters of residential real estate was under construction over that 11-month period. And as I have argued in the past, if China continues to expand its residential construction sector, there's a chance that the country will simply end up with more apartments than people. But I find that unlikely. When a country is building new apartments at such a grand scale, many questions related to sustainability must be answered. Because when it comes to the China property construction binge, there is a lot of math that simply does not add up. And this is a very big problem.

China has a problem of massive proportions. It has the mother of all credit-fueled property bubbles. This is a bubble so big that I struggle to find an example to use as a benchmark. The best way to describe this bubble is if the Japanese IZNOP business model continued to grow without a trigger breaking it down at the same rapid rate as it did during the 1980s, and it lasted all the way into the late 1990s. Or, imagine if the median property price in Miami and Los Angeles peaked before the 2006 property downturn at 15x-25x household incomes. That **is** China today. The median house price across a broad cluster of cities in China is astronomical. This is due to the manic-paced property price growth rate that involves property buyers outbidding one another over the better part of a decade. And on paper, it is clear that property investors in China do not give a damn about earning income from their property investments. It's all about capital gain.

City	Gross Rental Yield (2010-2012)
Shanghai	2.5%
Beijing	2.7%
Guangzhou	2.9%
Shenzhen	2.8%
Hangzhou	1.53%

The above table clearly suggests that property price speculation is the name of the game in China. Look at those measly returns on investment. By the time you calculate the net yield, investors aren't making any returns at all. Worse yet, you have property investors who would rather not rent out their investment properties and earn nothing because they want that apartment to be in impeccable condition to get the best price they can when they inevitably flip it to another buyer—the most speculative of strategies for a property investor.

Province	House price-to-income ratio
Hainan	25x
Beijing	22x
Zhejiang	22x
Fujian	20x
Guangdong	18x

As you can see in the table above, these are house price-to-income ratios across various regions in China. These are astronomical numbers. Compare these to Houston's 3.1x, and you can see the extent to which households in China are going to get their hands on a piece of property. But mathematically, there is simply no way whatsoever that the majority of homebuyers in China have the applicable means to save up just for a measly deposit for a home in China without taking on huge sums of debt relative to their incomes. Using Hainan province as an example, if the median property price grew by just 4%, the difference in price from the previous year would be the equivalent of an entire year's income. A property bubble has never burst in China before due to property investment being a relatively new open market for Chinese investors. We in the Western world are being told that the Chinese households are cashed up and buying houses using cash and sometimes small loans.

Country	House debt as a % of GDP
USA	85%
UK	101%
Japan	77%
China	32%

I think that it's highly unlikely that household debt in China is the equivalent of just 32% of GDP after more than a decade of house prices screaming up so high and so fast relative to incomes. But I will leave this argument for others to tussle about. In saying that, if we give more than a pinch of salt of seriousness to the data, it tells us that Chinese homebuyers are coming up with much bigger deposits for a home in comparison to what other homebuyers are paying around the world. But just 10 years ago Chinese workers were earning *less than one-third* of what they earn today. In short, it is very difficult to figure out how Chinese families—including retirees—have saved up enough money to make such large down payments on homes when property prices exceed 10x the household income in a country whose households weren't earning anywhere near what they are today over the last 20 years. Furthermore, property prices in China have shot up much faster over the last decade than they did in the United States, Ireland, and even Japan in their credit-fueled property bubbles. I firmly believe that there is a lot more household debt in China than we are being told. Another data point suggests the household debt-to-disposable-income ratio rose to 53% in 2012 from 31% in 2008. Once again, I would guess that the actual figure is far higher.

The Americans, Japanese, Irish, and Spanish raised their property prices to the heights they did before bursting through the use of excessive debt. I cannot see how the Chinese real estate market has so little debt in proportion to GDP. Furthermore, rich foreigners aren't rushing to buy houses across every corner of China like they are in a few global neighborhoods in and around central London and Manhattan.

Even though it is very common in China for parents in or nearing retirement to offload a significant proportion of their life savings (cash) to help their only child purchase a home, there remains, more often than not, still a massive proportion of mortgage debt for their son or daughter to pay off relative to what most middle-class Chinese residents are earning. And keep in mind the mass migration of citizens moving from the poorer farming areas of China to the more expensive cities. This could be compared to an employed Nebraskan farmer's minimum-wage-earning child moving to central London. How many Nebraskan households would be able to give a child a 60% deposit for an apartment in South Kensington, London? Hardly any! And if they could, would they? This is what is confusing about the whole property market in China. There is simply no way that many of these Chinese farming families could've saved anywhere near enough money to help a son or daughter to such an extent without excessive risk taking. Even the rents that offer investors no net yield are simply unaffordable in the cheaper outer suburbs of big Chinese cities when you consider the amount that most farmers would be able to save.

In the cities where incomes are higher, it is still hard to justify that there is as little debt as there apparently is. And 30% deposits aren't easy to come up with. In a place like Zhejiang province, the median family needs to save up the equivalent of 6.6x the household income just to make a 30% deposit to buy a home for their adult child. Even if the parents and the child are all chipping in, this is how it would hypothetically look to purchase a median home with very favorable and unusual circumstances that allow a homebuyer (the child) to gain access to debt.

Zhejiang Homebuyer (% of annual household income)	30% deposit	Leverage	Total
Son (Homebuyer)	1.3x	15.4x	16.7x
Parents	5.3x		5.3x
Total	6.6x	15.4x	22x

It seems mathematically impossible that the homebuyer could pay interest. The central bank interest rate at the People's Bank of China (PBOC) is 5.6%. Clearly homebuyers are charged a higher interest rate than that. Let's assume that by some miracle this median Chinese homebuyer has 70% of his disposable income (0.7x) to pay down debt on a loan 15.7x his income. The most interest this homebuyer could pay is 4.5%. This is not possible, considering China's interest rate environment. So what must be happening is that parents are making much larger contributions.

The only way I can see this system working is if married couples and parents of both partners throw everything they have toward the purchase of a property. This would reduce the overall loan size relative to income, and the debt payments would be split between the partners, which doubles the repayments made. This essentially halves everything and reduces the husband and wife's down payment.

Zhejiang Homebuyer	50% deposit	Leverage	Total
Husband & Wife (Homebuyer)	0.2x	5.5x	5.7x
Wife's Parents	2.65x		2.65x
Husbands Parents	2.65x		2.65x
Total	5.5x	5.5x	11x

In my opinion, it would be very unusual that a family (like the one represented in the above chart) outside of the wealthiest 10% of China's population would have the financial means to be able to buy a standard apartment in Zhejiang without having to throw in every cent of life savings just to make a 50% deposit. And for the farmers moving to Zhejiang Province . . . there's no chance. But even per the table above, if we assume that both husband and wife are income earners and they can allocate 70% of their incomes to mortgage repayments, there's still not much margin for error if they're paying 12% in annual interest. It seems a lot safer to rent in this type of economic environment. If one member of the couple loses his or her job, they will be forced to sell the home. There is no other country in the world where property buyers make such desperate attempts to get on the property ladder. These people take even more desperate measures than the Australians! So how are so many Chinese getting access to such levels of debt at a ratio that dwarfs house price ratios in almost every corner of the world?

Shadow banking is China's subprime

There are some awful similarities between the Chinese property bubble and the American credit-fueled property bubble, but on a much larger and riskier scale. Firstly, we know that, as in past credit-fueled IZNOP models, most homebuyers in China think that property prices will only rise. And because so many Chinese have made a fortune investing in this zero-sum game, the dominant expectation is that anyone who jumps into the property market in China will become rich. Not only that but the belief is that there is not much risk because if you can't pay your mortgage, the price of your property will have risen so much that in the worst case scenario you will still walk away with a profit. And because the official Chinese banking system has tight lending rules, homebuyers in China, like many Americans did pre-GFC, have taken on debt through what can be described as a second-tier lending market: Shadow Banking. But don't be fooled. Just because they call it "Shadow Banking" doesn't mean that Chinese homebuyers are walking into a pawn broker's shop to get debt. Shadow banks raise funds through the financial system and loan the funds out to homebuyers, businesses, and governments. And it wouldn't surprise me if there are a heap of 2006-style junk CDOs flying around.

These Chinese shadow banks offer those who invest in their funds a much higher interest rate than the rates offered by their state-sponsored banking counterparts. And they charge mortgage holders a much higher interest rate, so much so that the official interest rate in China doesn't so much affect how much a homebuyer will pay each month in interest because there's already a big spread in place between what banks and shadow banks offer deposit holders in interest. So many Chinese with cash prefer to invest in shadow banking products because they generally offer more than twice the interest. But as I argued in my previous book, the funds invested in the shadow banking system aren't secure investments. They're risky because the shadow banking system in China is off the government's balance sheet. It is very hard for a government to ever bail out a financial institution that has no formal relationship with its central bank. And that's where all the problems can occur.

High Risk

We often seem to forget that China is still a developing nation, and that its banking system is also still developing. It is exceptionally challenging for China's government to keep tabs on the shadow banking sector. It's also very hard to pinpoint precisely how much money is tied up in the shadow banking sector. The estimates range anywhere from 20% to 80% of GDP. Because there is such a variance in data, it would be worthless to attempt to figure out the breaking points of the Chinese shadow banking system. But we do know that these second-tier lending institutions must be holding very little capital on the sidelines, because it is my understanding that the interest rate spread between what they owe investors and what they lend is too slim to protect themselves should there be an economic downturn (e.g., paying 10% interest to the investor while charging 12% interest to the mortgage holder). And because the shadow banking system caters generally to those who can't get financing through a formal banking system that offers debt at a much lower interest rate, we can assume these shadow banks are financing people whom the prime banking system considers to be less credit-worthy. The less credit-worthy need or want financing, but are rejected by the prime banking sector. So they go through the alternative and more expensive loan channels. And the shadow banking system is there to pick up what the prime banking system rejects.

It's not just in home loans that this shadow banking system allocates huge sums of debt. The shadow banking system lends to every facet of the Chinese economy. And when it comes to corporate debt, China has a lot of it—more than any country should feel comfortable with having. In addition, the PBOC and the central government in China has done very little to try to slow down the corporate debt levels, which are rising at a stifling rate.

To better monitor shadow banking activities, the PBOC and central government would do well to build a regulatory framework that will be respected by its citizens, business leaders, and shadow bankers. This is no easy feat. Without concrete data, a society can easily get caught by surprise when an economy starts to lose steam. And with official Chinese debt levels relative to GDP rising at a rapid rate, it's better to know what debt exists rather than stay in the dark.

Year	2008	2010	2012	2014	2015 (est)
Total China Debt to GDP (%)	153%	195%	209%	236%	245%

As one can see, China's hypergrowth model now is 100% dependent on credit expansion. And if we narrow this data down a bit more, we'll see which sector of the Chinese economy is the culprit causing rising debt levels.

Year	2008	2010	2012	2014	2015 (est)
China Corporate Debt to GDP (%)	97%	125%	142%	167%	175%

The above table makes it clear that it is the corporate sector that is driving up debt levels in China. And fast! In 2008, China had roughly $4.3 trillion in corporate sector debt. By 2014, that number had screamed all the way up to $17.27 trillion. This is a 400% (4x) increase in the sum value of corporate debt in just seven years. If this trend was to continue over the next seven years, China would have more than $69 trillion in corporate debt. Once again, I highly doubt this will happen. But a 400% increase in debt versus 217% economic growth over the last seven years are insane numbers. We clearly see that Chinese economic growth is simply not keeping up with credit growth in the corporate sector. This is an IZNOP business model like I have never seen before.

China's corporate sector is even borrowing at a faster rate than the American government!

	Outstanding debt 2006	Outstanding debt 2014
U.S. Government Debt	$8.50 Trillion	$17.82 Trillion
China Corporate Debt	$4.30 trillion	$17.27 trillion

Where did this debt come from?

My biggest question of all is: Where on earth is all of this money coming from in the first place? How did China's banking system come up with another $12.9 trillion in the last seven years to lend to its corporate sector? The Chinese banking system (both formal and informal) simply wouldn't have been able to come up with such funds to lend without the help of the PBOC. This central bank must be printing money at a breakneck rate. And it is.

In 2002, the Fed, ECB, BOJ, and PBOC all had less than $1 trillion worth of assets on their balance sheet. By 2012?

Central Bank	Assets (2012)
BOJ	$1.8 Trillion
ECB	$3.5 Trillion
The Fed	$2.9 Trillion
PBOC	$4.5 Trillion

Between 2002 and 2012, the balance sheet of the PBOC grew by more than 818%. The Fed's balance sheet over the same period grew by half of that, and America had the mother of all economic downturns!

Where is the majority of this debt being invested? Well, considering that China consumed more cement in the last three years than the United States did in all of the last century, we can safely assume that this credit expansion has flowed right into infrastructure and housing development. Furthermore, manufacturers and exporters are taking on significant sums of leverage, which is of great concern.

It's no secret that the Chinese banking system regularly gets recapitalized by the PBOC. If it didn't, the Chinese banking system would've already collapsed several times over in the last 14 years. In other words, the Chinese banking system is an insolvent industry that regularly gets bailed out to keep the IZNOP business model from breaking down. Because if the banking system as a whole cannot lend more than it did the year before, China's economy will crash. And I'm not talking about an Irish-, American-, or Japanese-style crash. I'm talking about a double-digit hard landing as the economy attempts to find its floor. If the Chinese infrastructure and housing construction binge completely stopped tomorrow, theoretically 46% of its GDP would be wiped out instantaneously. What I fear is that China has constructed at such a fast rate that the country will run out of infrastructure to build. China has more airports, train stations, art galleries and, more importantly, housing than it will need for the next 20 to 30 years.

But we have to take our hats off to the Chinese for showing how mankind can transform a nation so quickly. This is one of the greatest human achievements of all time. When was the last time a country on planet Earth was able to complete its infrastructure and housing planning 20 years ahead of schedule? During the same amount of time that it took the relevant infrastructure planning authorities to debate and decide on whether Sydney should get a new single train line added to its existing network, entire metro systems (plural) were built in China. On the negative side, there are financial and economic consequences associated with building too much too soon. The first and foremost problem is that China is running out of things to build. Second, China's private sector economy has taken on too much risk. Thirdly, China has overbuilt. And lastly, history tells us that when Chinese investors get burned investing in domestic asset classes, they will likely walk away from investing in that particular asset class altogether.

Not every asset class in China is experiencing a bubble

China may have brewed the mother of all credit bubbles over the last seven years. But it has had one of the worst-performing stock markets in the world during the same time frame.

Year	2005	2007	2009	2011	2013
Shanghai Composite Index	1162	6039	1878	2680	2185

The table above depicts a pretty nasty stock market crash that has experienced no real recovery. While stock markets in Europe, America, and Japan have rebounded significantly since the GFC, China's did not. It has practically remained stagnant over the last several years. Even by November 2014, the Shanghai Composite Index was around 2450 points. In 2007, the P/E ratio of the index was more than 40x earnings. Today it is around 7x. On one hand, you have companies that are offering better earnings ratios than what you could ever find in the United States, Europe, or Japan. But on the other hand, when you know the amount of corporate debt that is out there, you know that the risk profile of the stocks on this stock market is very high. Furthermore you have a whole country of mom and pop investors who don't like to invest in the stock market after having been burned in the last crash and also because they think the Shanghai Composite Index stocks are rigged for the elite to make money.

If you look at the Shanghai Composite Index's performance since 2009, it's easy to see that (compared to the DAX, S&P 500, and the Nikkei) the Shanghai Composite Index could hardly be considered rigged. And if it is rigged, the riggers have done an exceptionally crappy job, considering that the market has hardly moved in the last several years. The S&P has almost tripled in the same period of time. But if the Shanghai Composite were to start swiftly rising for one reason or another, it *would* be a good signal that Chinese investors were pulling their money out of the property game and packing it into the local stock market. And that, Dear Reader, would be a very early and clear sign that the property bubble in China had reached bursting point.

What is also clear is that the money the PBOC prints doesn't impact the stock market like it does in other countries. So, in short, China has a very leveraged corporate sector and a stock market that gives a fair valuation of stocks relative to the risk taken. Furthermore, it's clear that the Shanghai Composite Index is not in a speculative state and it hasn't been since it last crashed. This, in my opinion, is a good indication of what investors in China do once they get burned. They walk away from investing into that particular asset class that burned them. So one day, when this credit-fueled property bubble bursts, which is looking like it could happen sooner than later, it will burn a whole lot more Chinese people than the number of people who got burned when the Chinese stock market crashed.

The Trigger

When it comes to China's economic structure, there are endless triggers that could break down the largest IZNOP business model in history. The property market is, in my opinion, the largest asset bubble in the world. Recently, the Chinese property market has begun to cool down. And we may be at the very early stages of the break down of the Chinese IZNOP business model. Property prices across most cities fell in November of 2014, and they are now down by 3% to 8% from their all-time highs.

Since this is a population that has made a one-way bet that property prices only rise, families are throwing in all of their life savings to guarantee that their children can own their own homes. Hence, there is practically no margin for error. On top of this, the new homebuyers are also taking on massive sums of debt in order to come up with enough money to purchase property in a bubble market. And with so many speculators in the property market, you also have a problem of vast proportions. If everyone is jumping into this property market in pursuit of capital gain and then everyone realizes that the market is insanely overpriced and goes down (like it has started to), China will have tens of millions of property investors all trying to pull out of the asset class at the same time. And as I argue in my previous book, the shadow banking system which funds a lot of debt in the housing market could find itself between a rock and a hard place.

Since the shadow banking system lends to both developers and homebuyers, you just need a small but healthy proportion of property developers to start to run out of money while constructing new dwellings for a problem to arise. The minute one of the larger shadow banking syndicates is unable to cover its losses and pay back its investors, the whole IZNOP system will break down. *Because this will create panic.* And if the collapse of the Shanghai Composite Index during the GFC is anything to go by, *it will be an incredibly hard landing*. If the shadow banking system hypothetically has $7 trillion in outstanding loans and just $200 billion in cash sitting on the sidelines for a rainy day, and then all the shadow banking investors want to pull their money out, there will be a run on the shadow banks at the same time that property owners can't sell their properties—and behold a credit crunch that the Chinese government and PBOC could never solve. This is a very serious problem that could make what the United States experienced in 2008 look like a small trip up.

This hypothetical scenario would be absolutely devastating for China. Worst of all, all data points suggest that such a scenario is extremely plausible when the property bubble there really does burst. Suddenly construction would come to an abrupt and absolute halt. Jobs would be lost on a colossal scale. Trillions of dollars would be wiped off the asset valuations of homeowners and developers and up to 46% of GDP would cease. And let's not forget the $17 trillion in corporate debt. If the shadow banking system is in the midst of a credit crunch, it won't lend money to anyone. Thus, every facet of the Chinese economy will be hit. And because homebuyers and developers are so credit hungry and dependent on credit, a lack of credit means that leveraged asset valuations will have nowhere to go and they'll depreciate very swiftly.

How could a central bank of a $9 trillion economy stop this from happening if a trigger is pulled? It cannot. It doesn't matter how much stimulus you give or how much money you print—when the IZNOP business model has already broken and the public stops investing into that particular asset class called real estate, all one can do is throw in the towel.

The Transition

I don't know how bad it will get in China when this property bubble bursts. But I do know that China has a shot of quickly transforming its economy. And if any country can navigate a rapid economic restructure, it's China! Although it's a "kick the can down the road" recommendation, the first priority would be to ease the pressure of a credit crunch while the economy goes into the greatest free fall the world has ever seen. And the way to do that is to focus on aspects of the economy that have been, by all accounts, relatively neglected.

First up? China's environment. China has one of the world's biggest pollution problems. Mind you, China is also one of the most beautiful countries on earth when there's no pollution hanging around. The only way I can see China somewhat softening the blow of a housing crash would be by rejuvenating its environment. China already is a big user of renewable energies, and I'm not talking about installing more wind turbines. But I do think the country could bring the health of the land and water back to the pristine shape that it once was before this country went on a construction binge. The rivers and lakes within China need to be cleaned up. This would take a lot of manpower. Rejuvenating the quality of water in China would improve China's ability to be more reliant on its own agricultural abilities, as well as providing cleaner drinking water. A national project of such a scale would cost trillions of dollars to do. But it could be the best investment China could ever make. And the beneficial knock-on effects would be priceless. It would significantly improve the quality of life and health for its citizens. There'd be growth in tourism too! With cleaner air and waterways, there is no doubt in my mind that China could become the world's most visited tourist destination. The history of this country is truly fascinating. It is indeed a country that every human should visit at least once in his or her lifetime.

The banking system

If construction in China comes to a grinding halt, the knock-on effects and economic shock to the global economy and financial system would be staggering. This could create another global credit crisis that would impact the more vulnerable banks around the world that are today highly exposed to the China growth story. And what does history tell us when trillions of dollars are stuck between a rock and a hard place? Stock markets crash! People stop spending and the cost of commodities become cheaper. Governments and world central banks are also forced to administer shots of morphine to ease the pain and buy some time so the economy can sort out its mess.

Some European banks have made a very big bet on the China growth story. Nobody has a crystal ball, but what would happen to the foreign banks and pension funds that are very dependent on the China growth story if China goes belly up? How does this impact a bank account deposit holder in the U.K. or elsewhere if their banks fail because they made bad investments in another country? More importantly, the banks in Europe were bailed out because they screwed up when investing in their own backyards. But will governments and central banks in Europe and the U.S. bail out banks that made bad bets on China? We will only know if the Yellens and Draghis of the world are forced to make such decisions. Systemic risk of the global financial system is definitely a given. But I would say there is much more systemic risk to the banking systems that were not as badly impacted in 2008 as were the American and European banks—particularly the Asian banks and the banking systems in countries that are 100% dependent on the China growth story. Once again, the American and Swiss banks are, as of 2014, the banks that have immediate cash on hand to cover the shortfalls of a serious global economic downturn. Where would Asian investors want to hold their money if the Asian banking system is looking ready to jump off a cliff?

The inflation/deflation impact

The absolute worst-case scenario for the global economy is if a massive amount of loan defaults occur across China's manufacturing sector. If this happens to such an extent that the majority of Chinese goods exporters cannot operate and export goods, the global economy will have a very serious problem, because the world is terribly dependent on the fluid supply of Chinese-made goods. If the Chinese manufacturing industry as a whole crumbles because of bad debts and fewer products are exported from China, global inflation could go through the roof. And as for my argument that global deflation (in $USD terms) is more likely in the near future, all bets are off. For example, if you own one of China's largest T-shirt manufacturing facilities and 80 of your 100 largest rivals within China go bust because they were living off of credit, are you going to charge more or less for a T-shirt? If suddenly every clothing brand around the world is knocking on your door because their existing Chinese suppliers went bust, and capacity-wise you can only supply so many T-shirts, you raise the price! Imagine the same scenario unfolding across thousands of industries! This essentially is the scenario that the world *must* avoid at all costs. Because if this scenario were to ever come to fruition, store shelves in consumer stores around the world would be empty for an intermediate period of time. But the cost of goods across a very broad range of business sectors would increase dramatically. Even if the price of oil and steel fell to record lows, central banks around the world would be forced to send interest rates sky-high in a relatively short time frame because inflationary forces would simply not be manageable without raising rates. We must never underestimate the truly important role that Chinese manufacturers play in this globally connected economy.

Alternatively, and just as importantly, if China's manufacturing industry doesn't take that big a hit, the deflationary pressures on the global economy (in $USD terms) could be significant. Excluding any geopolitical risk in the world, it could be assumed that if the Chinese economy comes to a halt, the price of oil would be coming down, which would make the cost of fuel cheaper not only in China but around the world. Furthermore, as there has been no country in the world so dependent on steel to fuel its hunger for GDP growth, we can only imagine the impact that global deflation would have if the cost of the prime ingredient China consumed at a massive scale to construct all the new infrastructure and housing over the last 15 years came crashing down. That ingredient? Iron ore. In $USD terms, if the cost of steel declines significantly on the back of plummeting iron ore prices, it can be all but guaranteed that the world is going to become a much cheaper place (in $USD terms). Even Chinese exporters could benefit from this. But the world becoming cheaper in $USD terms doesn't necessarily mean that the world outside America becomes cheaper when you factor in currency risk. Excluding Japan and Europe, inflation would be a given for most countries that do not peg their currency to the $USD. For example, if the Australian dollar were to drop by 20% against the $USD in the span of less than a month, there is a good chance the cost of imported goods would rise swiftly, creating inflation while America became a cheaper place for its citizens to live.

Ultimately, a very heavy price will be paid by those countries' economies that made one gigantic bet on the China growth story. I like to call them "the nouveau-riche states." These countries, particularly those in Asia-Pacific and the Latin American and African continents, have suddenly found this "new-found-wealth" on the back of betting the livelihoods of their economies on the hope that China's economy will only grow. And no other country in the Western world has made such a casino-like gamble on the China growth story while learning absolutely nothing from the failures of Japan, America, and Ireland than the country that I now call home.

Chapter Thirteen

Australia

Fool's Paradise

I'm just going to say it. Since returning to live in my homeland after a decade of traveling 150,000+ miles a year around the world, I have never seen a country (apart from China) whose citizens are so unknowingly caught up in a credit-fueled property bubble. Furthermore, never have I seen a central bank or politicians completely miss, or do nothing about, all the warning signs of an IZNOP business model. If anything, they bend over backwards by implementing policies to keep propping up the IZNOP. I've also never been to a country whose central bankers and government treasury forecast how much iron ore China will need in the next 20 years without using a calculator. Which country am I talking about? You guessed it! Australia.

Australia may be known for its great lifestyle, but let me tell you, this country is living in a Disneyland delusion. And as I argued in my previous book, *Australia: Boom to Bust*, this economy is 150% dependent on just three industries which I call the Three Pillars of the Australian Economy. The Banking, Mining, and Real Estate/Construction sectors, in total, make up roughly 37% of Australian GDP. After almost a quarter of a century without a recession, there are some serious economic debt-bomb skeletons hiding inside the closet of the Australian economy. But when society gets caught up in the myopia of an IZNOP business model, why bother checking the closets? Times are so good!

First, the Australian banking system is primarily a domestic-focused retail banking system. But by all mathematical accounts, the majority of the retail banks' balance sheets resemble the balance sheet of Lehman Brothers 15 months prior to its collapse. On top of this, the banking system has lent at an astronomical rate to homebuyers (sound familiar?). Finally, you have a mining industry, treasury, and central bank placing casino-like bets that China will continue to consume so much iron ore that, by 2030, the country will resemble the planet Cybertron in the Transformers cartoon.

On the back of this big bet on property and mining, the society, and those powerful enough to influence it, sincerely thinks that *"this time it's different."* So different that it could only leave a foreign observer absolutely bewildered. Particularly when it comes to real estate. The laughable attempts to justify why property prices in Australia are so high are what concerns me, because Australian society has now literally fallen for every excuse that was previously made to justify why Irish and Japanese house prices were rising so fast before they went bust. And no excuse has so hoodwinked the public more than the excuse that Australian central bankers, retail bankers, politicians, and other real estate pundits scream out into the world by way of their media-friendly associates at the mainstream newspapers and television stations.

Australia has a shortage of housing and land.

If you were to believe what Australian society is told by the local banking and real estate pundits, Australia does not have enough housing and developable land to house its population. Yes, that's right. With a population density of only 2.8 people for every square kilometer, Australia is the 223rd most densely populated country in the world. In other words, *there is hardly any population relative to the physical size of the country*. But this doesn't stop the pundits from telling the public that there's only so much land that can be used for construction. And do Australians actually believe there is a shortage of housing stock and land? You bet! Now, as I mentioned in the Japan Chapter, I could perhaps be convinced of this argument in a very high-density city like Tokyo. But this is Australia! *In Australia there are no Tokyos, Londons, or New Yorks!* Here are some humorous examples of Australia's "housing and land shortage."

Example One

Just over 233,000 people reside on the Northern Territory's (NT) 1,420,970 km2 land mass. That equates to just 0.17 people per square kilometer across the Territory. **There are more square**

kilometers in the NT than there are arms and legs of its residents combined. NT has arguably one of the lowest population densities on planet Earth. With 5.88 square kilometers of land for every resident of the Northern Territory, have these local residents fallen for such a myth that the NT has a land shortage? Oh, but they have! NT has more than three times the landmass of California. In Alice Springs (population 30,000), vacant land has recently been sold to a property buyer for twice the asking price (per square meter) of a vacant piece of land in the back hills of Malibu, California. As you may remember, Malibu is an extremely affluent suburb in the second-largest metropolitan area (by population) in the United States. The GDP of Los Angeles is roughly 50% of Australian GDP. The sixth-busiest airport in the world is just 35 minutes down the road from Malibu. Alice Springs? It's a very remote town right in the middle of Australia and as far away from the beach as you can get! What is there in Alice Springs? An airport that hosts seven departures a day, a few pubs, and an abundant and much-needed supply of insect repellant. And Malibu?

When land in the middle of what an American would call BFN costs twice as much as land in the hills of Malibu and other affluent neighborhoods in America, surely the alarm should be raised! Shouldn't the Reserve Bank of Australia (RBA) and federal politicians address the exorbitantly high cost of real estate? Apparently not.

Example Two

Sydney is Australia's largest city, with more than 4.7 million residents. By area, Sydney is one of the largest cities in the world. And believe me when I say it takes a very long time to drive from the eastern-most tip of Sydney to the western fringes.

The house price-to-income ratio of Sydney over the long term has been slightly more than 5x household income. Today, the house price-to-income ratio in Sydney is more than 10x household income. But when you break the data down suburb by suburb, you see something overwhelmingly insane. Check out a sample of suburbs in this 12,485 square-kilometer city and their suburban house price-to-income ratios for houses and apartments.

Sydney Suburb	Median House Price	Median Apartment Price	Median Household Income	Price to Income Ratio (House/Apt)	Distance from City Center
Bondi Beach	$1,845,000	$738,000	$96,512	19.11x/7.64x	9.4km
Cronulla	$1,375,000	$565,000	$75,660	18.17x/7.46x	30.4km
Manly	$1,906,000	$881,000	$108,368	17.58x/8.13x	14.7km
Strathfield	$1,673,000	$575,000	$76,440	21.89x/7.52x	13.6km
Liverpool	$530,000	$315,000	$47,944	11.05x/6.57x	40.6km
Bankstown	$628,000	$380,000	$49,400	12.71x/7.6x	29.9km
Hurstville	$1,130,000	$575,000	$59,124	19.11x/ 9.73x	24.7km

These house-price ratios bewilder me! This is an enormous rise in property prices from the 5x price-to-income ratio that was the case before the bubble started to inflate. But like Alice Springs, there's an apparent shortage of buildable land in Sydney, and property buyers are aggressively outbidding each other to get their hands on property. Sydney is one of the 10 most expensive cities in the world if you're looking to buy a square meter of real estate. To get a little perspective, Sydney is about as densely populated as the major Texan cities, which have much cheaper real estate markets. And when you look at the nine other most expensive property markets in the world per square meter, you can really see how Sydney sticks out like a sore thumb.

City	Density (inhabitants per km2)	City	Density (inhabitants per km2)
Monaco	18,005	Singapore	7,540
Hong Kong	6,544	Moscow	4,581
London	5,354	New York	10,725
Geneva	12,261	Sydney	380
Paris	3,697	Shanghai	3,799

So there you have it. Nine exceptionally densely populated cities and then sticking out like Shaquille O'Neal standing with a group of third graders . . . Sydney. If Sydney was as densely populated as London, it would have a population of 66.8 million people living within its city limits. That's almost three times the total population of the entire country of Australia! Sydney simply shares no physical or economic characteristics with the other expensive property markets of the world. But Sydney's property market *does* share exceptionally similar characteristics with some of the world's most famous property bubbles prior to their collapse. Miami, Los Angeles, Dubai, and Dublin come to mind.

But Sydneysiders love that Sydney is seen as an expensive place to live. The locals sincerely believe that global business revolves around what happens in Sydney. I'm sure the Irish know exactly what I'm talking about. And since moving back home, I've quickly realized that Australia's most popular sports are no longer cricket, rugby, and Aussie Rules football. The most popular sports in Australia today? Jabbering about real estate and keeping up with the Jones's.

Whether you live in one of the wealthier or not so well-off neighborhoods of Sydney, there is simply no escaping insanely high property prices relative to what the masses earn. And unlike the U.K. and the U.S., there are strict restrictions regarding what properties foreigners can and cannot purchase. Only newly built dwellings and vacant land earmarked for construction can be purchased by a foreigner. All existing homes are exclusively reserved for Australian residents. So the impact of foreign buyers could not be what is broadly driving up the high price of real estate, whether in Sydney, Melbourne, or Alice Springs. The factor that has driven property prices to the heights they are today all across Australia is the IZNOP business model. The same model that was adopted by the Irish, the Japanese, the Americans, and the Spanish. But all the warnings have simply been totally ignored. Australians simply think that this time it's different.

Those warning about the credit-fueled property bubble are ignored

As one of very few Australians trying to raise the alarm of a credit-fueled property bubble, I can tell you that you go largely ignored. Unlike those who tried to warn of the credit-fueled property bubbles in Ireland and America in 2006, alarm ringers in Australia aren't involved or allowed to join in the debate. And compared to the hundreds of mainstream journalists in Australia who have the power to provide Australians with an objective view on the current state of the property market and the country's banking system, to the best of my knowledge there are only three or four of them who are jumping up and down trying to get the debate rolling in Australia regarding this most sensitive of topics. They are of the younger generations of journalists, not the old-school "Sydney property market is playing catch-up" journalists. To put it into perspective, and unless I am seriously mistaken, the Australian Treasurer Joe Hockey has only been asked twice in the last two years by journalists if Australia is experiencing a property bubble. Those two journalists, Bloomberg's William Pesek and CNBC's Amanda Drury, are *non-Australian-based* journalists. And on both occasions, Mr. Hockey has outright denied that Australia is experiencing a property bubble, let alone one that has been fueled by toxic sums of debt. I was attending the Bloomberg Business Summit in Sydney in September of 2014 when Joe Hockey responded to Pesek's credit-fueled housing bubble question. Hockey's response?

> *It's just an easy mantra for international commentators and for analysts based overseas to say, 'Well, there's a bit of a housing bubble emerging in Australia.' That is a rather lazy analysis because fundamentally we don't have enough supply to meet demand.*

I guess that makes me a lazy Australian-born foreign commentator living on the southern beaches of Sydney. And I'm guessing Joe Hockey, like the previous Australian treasurer Wayne Swan, never bothered to look at the datasets that suggest unequivocally that Australia has indeed a credit-fueled property bubble. Nor have they bothered to benchmark Australia against failed IZNOPs . . . Oh well.

But still there are some of the finest "local" economic researchers and academics in the country also sending the same warnings, all which have been largely ignored—Australian economics professors and analysts such as Steve Keen and Tony Locantro, for example. There are the economics bloggers for Prosper Australia and the Macrobusiness.com.au website also warning about excessive credit inflating a highly toxic property bubble. Overseas there's a whole wealth of analysts, such as Jesse Colombo, Harry Dent and Paul Gambles. Then there are Paul Egan and Philip Soos, the co-authors of "Bubble Economics," who have written the most compelling research document in Australian history on the domestic real estate market. No other researchers have done as much in-depth analysis to prove, beyond a shadow of a doubt, that the Australian property market is in the midst of the largest property bubble on record—making "expert" claims of justified pricing seem laughable. Still, the mainstream media Down Under have all but ignored their work. You would think that their 800-page tome would be the catalyst for a real debate by injecting some common sense notions into the heads of local politicians and central bankers. But the Australian political and financial elite, like their Irish counterparts in the recent past, have chosen to ignore valuable research that clashes with the official narrative.

In fact, the majority of economists interviewed by the Australian mainstream media work for major Australian financial institutions—the very financial institutions that have fueled the Australian housing market with an enormous sum of debt! Are these economists telling Australians that there is a credit-fueled housing bubble? *Of course they're telling Australians that no housing bubble exists!* What do the most trusted names in Australian economics tell Australians? That there is a housing shortage! What idiotic irresponsibility!

No matter what a politician from any side of politics has tried to bring to public attention over the last decade, they will never debate amongst themselves whether Australia has a credit-fueled property bubble. But what they will do is find ways to keep the IZNOP business model from breaking down. And to be quite frank, they have done an excellent job in doing so through implementing very favorable policies that stimulate the price of real estate. And these policies work because you have a public that has been completely fooled and is caught up in the IZNOP. However, as history tells us, the bigger an IZNOP gets, the bigger the blow when it breaks.

Today, the Australian property market is valued at more than $5 trillion. In 2013, in the state of New South Wales, the average property buyer borrowed more in sum *(just the mortgage alone equivalent to 7.6x income)* than an average New Yorker paid for a piece of property in total. And today, more loans than ever are interest-only loans, wherein the mortgage holder only pays interest on the loaned amount rather than paying both interest and principal. In addition, property investors today make up 50% of all property buyers. And since hardly any Australians have the cash to buy a property outright, they go to the bank, take out an 80%+ mortgage, and risk everything they have to be a part of a highly regarded club. That's why the Australian lenders mortgage insurance company Genworth generated—in a country the size of Australia—more than $422 million in gross written premiums in the first three quarters of 2014 alone. If there wasn't so much risky lending, a company like this wouldn't exist, let alone one that would never be able to cover its book of policies if the housing market did actually crash in Australia.

So what is the Reserve Bank of IZNOP doing to stop this out of control property market?

Date	March 2012	December 2012	August 2013	November 2014	February 2015
Interest Rate	4.25%	3%	2.5%	Still 2.5%	2.25%

Talk is talk and data is data. What is the RBA doing to stop this out of control property market? As per the table above, nothing! To the contrary, the RBA does all it possibly can within its powers to stop the property bubble from bursting. And here is the evidence in four simple sentences:

1. Property prices are at record highs.
2. Mortgage lending is at an all-time high.
3. Interest rates are at record lows.
4. Housing credit and property price growth are consistently rising faster than wages and inflation.

In my previous book, I forecasted the likelihood of Australia's IZNOP credit-fueled property bubble breaking down. Because interest rates in Australia today are at an emergency low 2.5%, and property prices and lending rates are as high as they are, there isn't much chance that interest rates could fall to near-zero. This is because the $AUD would simply collapse. That could mean that when this IZNOP business model breaks down, the RBA will have significantly less firepower than its foreign counterparts had when their IZNOP models crashed to the ground. But then again, property prices crashing from a higher interest rate level didn't help those central banks either.

Central Bank	Interest rate before IZNOP model crashed	Interest rate after IZNOP model crashed	Interest rate difference
The Fed	5.25%	0.25%	5%
ECB	4.25%	1%	3.25%
BOJ	6%	0.5%	5.5%

As for Australia, the RBA has already dropped interest rates significantly to stop the credit-fueled property bubble from bursting. It is hard to slash interest rates from bubble peak to collapse when you only have a spare 2.5% interest to utilize and your currency is not the most important in the world. If interest rates in Australia are already at record lows, when property prices tumble *(with hypothetically no impact to the currency)*, if interest rates were dropped it would continue to crush those who live off interest from the bank. But the RBA would have to also manage inflation, because the $AUD would depreciate much faster than the RBA would like. This could actually force the RBA to raise interest rates if the IZNOP model breaks down.

Although a bit late to the party, the American and Japanese central bankers at least tried to cool off the housing market as prices were skyrocketing. In Sydney, property prices have climbed by 14% over the 2013/14 financial year. That's more than a $100,000 price gain in 12 months! A 10% average price growth was recorded across Australia. The average home in Australia is valued at over $550,000! The average asking price for a house in Sydney in the second week of November 2014 was almost $1 million, with a median house price being well in excess of $830,000. However, the median household income in Sydney is $75,000. Interest rates have been at record lows, property prices have shot up, and banks are lending at a very toxic rate to homebuyers. And what has the RBA done? It has done *nothing*. And in most Australian rental markets, investors are renting out their investment properties at a loss. Because of the highly leveraged nature of the property investment market, property investors in a city like Melbourne cannot cover their costs with rental revenue. For example, the rent in Melbourne simply does not cover the mortgage costs unless you only take out a mortgage equivalent to 34% or less of the purchasing price of a property. Like the Chinese property investors in China, Australian property investors do not seem to care about rent. They only care about capital gain. And this will come back to haunt an economy that is so dependent on property prices only rising.

Sydney and Melbourne, the two largest cities in Australia, make up roughly 38% of Australia's total population. And they are the two biggest property bubbles in the country relative to incomes. Melbourne seems to have surpassed the 8x income barrier and Sydney is now well above 10x. When close to 40% of a countries population is living in a ridiculously overpriced property market, you would think that the RBA governor would raise interest rates! As data from American property researchers Demographia suggests, of the 37 largest cities and towns in Australia, only four of them have a lower median house price than Chicago, Illinois. Chicago is the third-largest city in the United States. And many of these cities and towns in Australia are remote towns in the middle of BFN. There's a pretty good chance that a small house in the-middle-of-nowhere Australia is more expensive than what half the residents of Chicago are paying for their homes. Once again, you would think that the RBA, more particularly its governor, Glenn Stevens, would have taken some sort of action to make housing more affordable back in 2008 when the property bubble should have burst alongside the other global IZNOP property bubbles. But Australia can thank golden ticket China for its "purchase all the iron ore Australia could dig from the ground"-style stimulus package.

By 2013, as became apparent that investment into the mining sector was at its peak, what did the RBA governor want? He wanted more Australians to get in the property game and build more houses to stimulate the construction sector of the Australian economy. As the members of the RBA also argue that Australia has a "lack of land," the population believed this central bank and its bankers and went on a credit-fueled property spending binge to get in the property game. Since new homebuyers and property investors have put their faith in the RBA's view that there is a housing shortage, they think they can't lose. Is Australia, a country of just 23.5 million people, not building enough housing?

New Housing Starts	Texas & California Combined	Australia
2001	258,743	139,446
2003	327,567	170,658
2005	372,554	154,560
2007	229,808	154,961
2009	101,951	142,066
2011	110,621	155,148
2013	172,746	168,424

Texas is one of the fastest growing states in the United States with a population of 26.5 million people. California, the most populous state in America, has 38.3 million people. These two states combined contain 64.8 million people. And in four of the last five years, a country with a population of just 23.5 million people has had more new housing starts. Doesn't sound like a housing shortage to me! But it does sound like there's an oversupply of debt available to homebuyers which creates artificial demand for real estate.

As California and Texas combined has 2.7x the population of Australia, how would the previous table look pound for pound if Australia's population was also 64.8 million?

New Housing Starts	Texas & California Combined	Australia (with same population as CA & TX combined)
2001	258,743	384,514
2003	327,567	470,580
2005	372,554	426,191
2007	229,808	427,296
2009	101,951	391,739
2011	110,621	427,812
2013	172,746	464,420

Relative to scale, Australia has overbuilt California and Texas combined even through the American property boom before the GFC occurred, and still there is the claim Australia doesn't have enough housing. California—the state that had one of the biggest construction booms in American history before the GFC—was still building at a slower rate than Australia consistently has been relative to population over the last 14 years. Every year! The population growth of Texas is faster than Australia's and has a slightly higher population—and they build nowhere near as much housing as Australia does. But in Australia, pundits love to use Texas as an example of a part of the world that over-constructs, while local Texan governments regularly release land for construction, hence, low land prices.

Apparently in Australia, every single local government in every single city, town, village, and desert doesn't release enough land to build on, which keeps the price of land extremely high. But when I actually drive around Sydney and the southern beaches of Sydney where I live, there is a wealth of new real estate developments—and even suburbs—being created out of thin air.

. . and vacant land!

These Australian property pundits are essentially lying to the local inhabitants. As Paul Egan and Philip Soos suggest, Australia is building one new dwelling for every 1.8 new residents. In Texas, the figure is closer to 2.3 new residents for every newly constructed home. The bulk of these new residents in Australia are either foreign university students, working holiday makers, long-term holiday makers and new-born babies. Hardly any of which would have the monetary means to purchase a piece of Australian real estate. Australia therefore will have an excess supply of housing the day the IZNOP business model breaks down. Those living beyond their means in vain attempts to "keep up with the Jones's" will eventually be forced to offload their properties in a market absent of property buyers as it drops into a sharp nose dive.

The real problem

Just as with the Irish and Japanese property bubbles in the past, while the powerful local central bankers, politicians, and real estate and banking pundits argue that a shortage of housing and an overwhelming demand are driving the price of property higher, there is a masking of the real reason as to why property prices in Australia cost twice as much relative to incomes back when the bubble started brewing more than 15 years ago: *The oversupply of toxic debt.* Talk about a country that hasn't bothered one bit to use history as a guide that shows what inevitably goes wrong when too much debt is pumped into one particular asset class. As I illustrated in the GFC trigger chapter, unless the Australian banking system, year in and year out, can lend more to homebuyers than it did the previous year, the bubble will inevitably burst.

By all mathematical calculations, in a property market where foreign buyers make up less than 7% of all property purchases, there is no way that the overwhelming majority of Australian households would have anywhere near the means to buy houses without acquiring abnormally massive sums of debt. On top of that, it is near impossible for first-time homebuyers to come up with enough savings even for a deposit on a home. So their parents are helping out beyond the stretch of wisdom. Did this country not learn anything at all from the mistakes of others? I know Australia is on the other side of the world, but it does have the Internet! It isn't hard to research past failures of countries that have adopted the IZNOP business model! Look at the following table measuring land price growth in the major Australian cities from 2001 to 2011. Percentage-wise, Japan's land bubble as a whole didn't come close to the height that Australian land prices have risen to. By 2001, land prices were already fast on the rise after property prices had taken off from the median in 1998.

Land Price per m2	December 2001	December 2011	%Increase
Sydney	$316	$533	169%
Melbourne	$132	$400	303%
Brisbane	$118	$398	337%
Adelaide	$125	$480	384%
Perth	$146	$527	361%
Hobart	$49	$225	459%

Roughly half of the towns in Ireland's out-of-control property bubble saw similar growth in land prices. And relative to population, Ireland had more new immigrants arriving into their country during the boom years than the number of immigrants entering Australia. And yet the RBA has brought interest rates to record lows, even though Australia is not in a recession.

The banking sector

As for the banking sector? It's one big IZNOP. After what happened in 2008 in the U.S., I never thought that a regulator of a domestic Western banking system would let its banks run free lending enormous sums of mortgage debt to the masses. But in Australia, the RBA thinks it's okay for Australian banks to lend the most unusual of amounts of debt to homebuyers and property investors—so much so that the rest of the economy doesn't have that much debt to share. There is roughly $1.9 trillion worth of loans made to the Australian private sector, and $1.53 trillion is household debt of which 90% is mortgage debt. Talk about a banking system that has made a one-way bet that house prices will only go up!

The Commonwealth Bank (CBA), the National Australia Bank (NAB), Westpac (WBC), and the Australia and New Zealand Banking Group Limited (ANZ) are the four largest banks in Australia (AKA, the Big Four). As per the table below, you can see that the balance sheets of some of the major Australian banks look eerily similar to that of a big investment bank that went bust in the GFC—and they look nothing like an ultraconservative Swiss bank.

Bank	Total Cash $Billions	Total Long-Term Debt $Billions	Total Assets $Billions	Cash vs. Assets Ratio	Cash as % of assets	Cash-Debt Ratio	Cash as % of Long-Term Debt
Bank 1: CBA (2013)	12,608	117,99	753,876	59.8x	1.67%	9.36x	10.69%
Bank 2: NAB (2013)	38,306	122,744	808,427	21.1x	4.74%	3.20x	31.21%
Bank 3: WBC (2013)	9,862	104,88	696,603	70.6x	1.42%	10.63x	9.40%
Bank 4: ANZ (2013)	39,129	91,57	702,991	18.0x	5.57%	2.34x	42.73%
Bank 5: Zurich Cantonal Bank (2013)	26,041	54,54	144,673	5,6x	18,0%	2,09x	47.75%
Bank 6: Lehman Brothers (2007)	20,029	123,15	691,063	34,5x	2,90%	6,15x	16.26%

When I look at the above table and compare the balance sheets of the four major Australian banks to a safe Swiss bank like the Zurich Cantonial Bank or the highly leveraged Lehman Brothers 15 months prior to its collapse, I would say the Australian banks are highly leveraged institutions. Particularly WBC and CBA. Anything on a balance sheet that looks, sounds, or smells like Lehman should raise alarm bells. And in Australia's case, two major banks hold less cash in their own banks accounts but hold more assets than Lehman Brothers did fifteen months prior to its collapse. But in Australia, nobody really thinks the banks are dangerously undercapitalized apart from a small handful of people—and by small handful, I mean literally 90 or 100 people out of 23.5 million!

Basel = Useless

Egan and Soos point out that Australian banks only hold around $1.50 of capital for every $100 extended for outstanding home loans (a 1.5% capital ratio). This leaves the Australian banking fraternity with a tiny margin for error. However, the banks have the utmost confidence in their optimistic assessments of creditworthiness! And the banking pundits and politicians consistently "stay on message," informing citizens that the banking system is firmly capitalized, and well-placed to weather a financial crisis without extraordinary measures.

You may be wondering why the banks can maintain such a thin safety buffer to withstand defaults. According to the Basel agreements that bind all major global banking institutions, banks may make their own internal (opaque) assessments of the future risk of default for home mortgagers. In Australia, the Big Four banks are particularly fond of this method, with the vast majority of housing loans in the mortgage portfolio using the internal ratings-based (IRB) approach that allows estimates of probability of default (PD), loss given default (LGD) and exposure at default (EAD). This is then combined with estimates of expected and unexpected future losses (EL, UL), informed by historical statistics, to determine how much capital is needed for a specified credit exposure. Critically, the basic formula for capital held = mortgage asset (loan) value x Basel III 8% regulatory requirement x risk-weighting. Thus, banks are routinely artificially lowering their estimates of mortgager default and their likely credit exposure and losses in the event of a downturn, which generates far lower-risk weights than accepted in the standard approach.

This is evident when the average risk-weight for mortgages in the sector is closer to 40%, yet it remains firmly in the mid to late teens for the Big Four banks. This means that instead of a true 8% capital ratio proudly touted by Basel, the mortgage portfolio is barely into the single digits. The additional benefit of this approach for banks is that additional capital is freed up for further lending, particularly when banks assess that an upwards, material change in the value of the mortgage book has occurred. Banks are further incentivized by this approach, because highly leveraged lending structures also increase the relative return on capital.

The upshot of all this is that even when a homebuyer has tenuous work circumstances and limited equity in his home, rarely are risk-weights assigned that reflect the significant risk attached to the loan, that is, approaching 100%. Like the situation described in the chapter on the GFC trigger, the mortgager is still considered credit-worthy and low-risk, even if living from paycheck to paycheck. The future inability to repay the loan within a short period following job loss is rarely considered by "prudent" lending institutions. This form of recklessness and distorted perceptions are what caused the GFC in the first place, with irrational exuberance in the financier class being a primary trigger! Incomprehensibly, Australian regulators do not question the longevity of this lending model. Instead, they have helped to form a false impression portraying banks as safe and having low thresholds for risk. Countering this, the household debt-to-income ratio and a host of other metrics have risen sharply, threatening to test the validity of those assessments in the very near term.

Year	Household debt-to-income ratio (Australia)
1993	56%
2003	93%
2013	150%

Australian household debt-to-income ratios have almost tripled in the last 20 years. Only a small number of Western countries have outdone what the Aussies are doing today when it comes to *rapid* growth in household debt. Ireland, Spain, and the Netherlands come to mind. And from 2014-15, banks have been lending at such a toxic rate to homebuyers that this number could only be higher. On top of this, close to $450 billion of outstanding debt are interest-only loans involving property buyers who are speculating that property prices will only rise. That is more than double the sum value of interest-only debt in the Australian property market since 2008. And the only way that the property buyers with interest-only loans can pay back the bank is if they sell the asset they borrowed against. So the Australian banking system has all but bet the financial livelihoods of their financial institutions—indeed, of a country—that property prices will only rise. The sum value of outstanding housing credit in Australia has jumped by 466% in just 14 years. Inflation over the same period was just 51%. In other words, between 1999 and 2013, housing credit was rising at a rate of 913% faster than inflation. But Australians don't seem to have a problem with this. Because the mortgage default rate is as high as Ireland's was back in 2005— in other words, very low . . because the IZNOP model is working its magic. So much for Basel agreements keeping the financial system safe!

And because the four largest banks in Australia each holds assets the equivalent of 45% to 49% of Australian GDP on their balance sheets, it wouldn't be as easy to bail out these banks as it was for the Fed and American Treasury to bail out its banking system. To put it into perspective, Lehman Brothers held roughly the equivalent of 5% of American GDP on its balance sheet. How could a country with a much smaller economy bailout four banks the actual size of Lehman Brothers if crunch came to crunch? And you can safely assume that when a country like Australia has four primarily domestic-focused retail banks that are all ranked in the top 30 banks in the world by market capitalization, one of the following is going on:

- Each bank in its own right has at the exact same time figured out the ultimate algorithm to never-ending financial prosperity.

Or

- They are all doing something very risky.

And when I look at the balance sheets of the Australian banks, I would say they are doing something incredibly risky. *They feed the IZNOP business model the debt*. On top of this, smaller lenders are offering 100% financing to young homebuyers as long as their parents put up their houses as collateral. And with the equivalent of American subprime loans flooding the marketplace, history is telling us that the Australian real estate market is caught up in the mother of all credit-fueled IZNOP models. Australian society has absolutely no clue of the real-world risks they have taken to get property prices to where they are. And when the Australian IZNOP model breaks down, many Australians will lose everything they have and more. And the banking system will either go down in flames or cost the Australian government hundreds of billions—at worst more than $1 trillion of RBA-printed money—to save the system or nationalize it. And in the worst-case, Australia could be left with nothing more than an $AUD that resembles a peso.

Australian politicians have no clue

Every several years, Australia's federal politicians have passed legislations to continue to prop up the IZNOP business model. This has been achieved through providing first-time homebuyers grants to the tune of $7,000 to $14,000 to purchase their first home. A few years later, Australia allowed those who manage their own retirement funds to use their life savings to purchase investment properties by borrowing against their retirement savings. And now what do Aussie politicians want to do to stop the credit-fueled property bubble from bursting? Let first-time homebuyers withdraw money from their retirement funds to come up with deposits for homes in what is the most expensive real estate market in the world. Australian Senator Nick Xenophon is an independent senator who is pushing this legislation through parliament. Funnily enough, Senator Xenophon himself owns several investment properties. And like Senator Xenophon, the overwhelming majority of politicians are also in the property game. Combined, of the 563 properties owned by Australia's 226 federal politicians, more than 312 of them are investment properties. It is hands down the greatest asset class owned by Australian politicians. Like the RBA bankers, politicians are by far the most docile of economists this world has seen in a long time. Europe copying Japan's recovery strategy is one thing. Australia copying the IZNOP credit-fueled property bubble models that got Japan and Ireland in a mess in the first place is another.

I stand by the prediction I made in April of 2014 that, before the end of 2017, the credit-fueled Australian property bubble will collapse, leaving at least one major bank in Australia either bankrupt, bailed out, or nationalized by the Australian government. And if one major Australian bank cannot lend to homebuyers, neither can the rest of them. There are triggers simply everywhere to bring this IZNOP business model crashing down to earth. Australia is a net importer of mortgage debt. The IZNOP model breaks down if the wholesale lenders in New York and London stop lending to the Australian banking system. The country has already exhausted all of its own deposits to prop up the mortgage market the way Australia has. Year after year, the banking system has to lend more to new homebuyers than they did the year before to keep the IZNOP model moving along. And if one major lending institution is unable to do that, by all mathematical accounts, the credit-fueled property bubble runs out of enough debt to fuel more price growth. And the Australian central bankers and politicians who've been waving their pom-poms in the air cheering this property price growth on will be left with one heck of a mess. Unfortunately, it will be those who were responsible and saved money who will inevitably foot the recovery bill. Australia may not have the next Google startup in its sights, but it does have the next Lehman Brothers.

Iron Ore

The Chinese are slowly but very surely coming to terms with the reality that they can't continue to consume iron ore the way they have been for the last several years. Slowly but surely, this will be one of the main triggers that will breakdown the Australian IZNOP model. And from the looks of it, my forecast that the spot price of iron ore per metric ton (MT) will reach as low as $20 before the end of 2017 is on track! Mining is the backbone of the Australian economy. More particularly, iron ore is the largest export to come out of Australia and the majority of every ounce of ire ore dug from the ground goes to China.

Country	January 2014 Iron Ore exports (metric tons)
South Korea	4.383 million
Japan	4.778 million
China	39.674 million

As you can see in the table above, of the 49 million metric tons of iron ore that was exported from Australia in January 2014, close to 40 million went to China. Japan and Korea's monthly iron ore intake from Australia is only a fraction of China's. And India will never be able to match China's growth in terms of construction. There's simply too much red tape in India to get the construction train rolling.

Date	April 2010	February 2011	February 2013	October 2014
Iron Ore Spot Price (MT)	$172.10	$187.18	$154.64	$81.00

Australia's backbone is looking extremely shaky. In November 2014, the spot price of iron ore fell to just below $69 MT. This price means that only two iron ore miners are now making money.

Iron Ore Supplier	Break-Even Spot Price (MT) Sept 2014
Rio Tinto	$45
BHP	$50
Fortescue Metals	$74
Mount Gibson Iron	$78
BC Iron	$81
Atlas Iron	$85

Here is the problem for these miners. Apart from the fact only two of the 10 largest miners are making real profits, China's economy has yet to really sneeze. When I mean sneeze, I mean property investors en masse heading for the hills and every second house in China being up for sale. We are close to that becoming a reality, but not there just yet. When that happens, it is all but certain that the spot price of iron ore will "really" collapse, because there is nowhere else in this world for all this newly extracted iron ore to go to. Japan and Korea can't all of the sudden need 5x more supply of iron ore. And just as likely, you or I, alongside every single person on the planet, will not be consuming 5x more steel as an end consumer anytime soon. Australia will essentially be left with all of these holes in the ground that cost an absolute fortune to dig. Mass sums of debt was required to build this large natural resources operation. I would be very surprised if the majority of creditors who backed these large scale projects in Australia will ever see their money returned with interest.

SKYFALL

Even though the mining giants of Australia have significantly brought down their extraction costs, it's been done through increasing volumes of iron ore extracted. So, in one sense they're bringing down their extraction costs, but in another sense, when demand for iron ore comes to a grinding halt and miners try to reduce supply to raise the spot price of iron ore higher, their extraction costs will increase accordingly. Here's a simple hypothetical example: if it costs your mining operation $1 million per year to operate and you extract only one MT of iron ore, your extraction cost is $1 million per MT. If that same mine was to extract 20,000 MT of iron ore instead of one MT, the extraction cost would now be $50 per MT. If the hypothetical mining operation reduces how much iron ore it extracts from the ground from 20,000 MT to 15,000 MT to try to help push the price of iron ore higher, the extraction cost would be $66 per MT, and it would be $100 per MT if the mine goes down to 10,000 MT per year. So, on the back of calculator-free forecasting of how much iron ore China will consume in the future, the Australian mining industry will be left in ruins, creating what I would call a SKYFALL scenario that will rip through the heart of the Australian economy. Because when a single dollar of debt in Australia is not allocated to real estate, more likely than not, that particular dollar of available debt ends up in the hands of a leveraged mining company.

Australia is definitely a country that has managed throughout the last two decades to dodge a lot of economic bullets. Having the right product (iron ore) to sell at the right time simply came down to luck, and Australia has definitely been the lucky country for sometime. But by all mathematical accounts, Australia is quickly running out of luck—it has one of the biggest IZNOP business models that will sooner than later breakdown. Australian central bankers and politicians have made a bet on land prices only rising on the back of a once-in-a-lifetime natural resources boom. Or, as the bloggers at the MacroBusiness website say: "a houses and holes economy."

And with society caught up in the IZNOP, it's all but certain that Australians have embraced the same business model that took down the Irish and Japanese economies, but they're expecting a different result. In my opinion, there is no better example of a country caught up in the IZNOP model than Australia on the back of a one-way bet. But the country is not alone.

The commodity club of nations

Unfortunately for the global economy, Australia is not the only country in this world that made a large bet on never-ending Chinese economic growth. Canada, Brazil, New Zealand, and half of the African countries have been great beneficiaries of the China growth story and also have IZNOP business models that will breakdown once China's IZNOP model breaks down. Brazil, in particular, has taken great lengths to expand not only its mining operations, but its upstream oil and gas operations by venturing well offshore from the beautiful beaches of Ipanema and Copacabana. As anyone knows, it isn't cheap to build a large-scale offshore drilling operation. Worst of all is if it's an operation that may never make a profit as the spot price per barrel of oil continues to decline. OPEC is digging its heels into the ground by not reducing production on the back of dropping oil prices. In other words, OPEC is trying to throw their global rivals out of business. And unfortunately for Brazil and its oil company, Petrobras, OPEC nations have the means and the money to ride out the storm versus its overseas rivals. And let's not forget one of OPEC's biggest rivals—Russia, which is currently taking an economic beating. Pressured now with geopolitical risk, the Russian economy needs oil prices to remain high. Low oil prices make it exceedingly difficult for oil and gas producers to pay down their $USD debts.

On top of heavy investment into the oil and gas industry by emerging nations, as a whole, many are spending a great deal in nation building on the backs of their new-found prosperity. The one-way bet these nations have made that China will continue to deliver large sums of foreign-derived income has given them a dangerous false sense of comfort that allows them to invest heavily in fixed asset investments as a proportion of their GDPs. This is particularly true of nations in and around Asia.

Fixed Asset investment (2012)	Proportion of GDP
Indonesia	33.2%
Thailand	28.5
Vietnam	28.2%
Sri Lanka	28.9%
South Korea	26.7%
Hong Kong	26.4%
Australia	28.5%

Many nations across Asia have been piggybacking off of China's new-found wealth. I fear that many Asian nations will, like Australia, inevitably feel the full force when China's IZNOP model breaks down. Because essentially, many Asian nations have IZNOPs of their own. And property investors all across Asia are making shameful yields on their investments

City	Gross Rental Yield (City Center)
Taipei	1.39%
Seoul	2.53%
Hong Kong	3.01%
Singapore	3.89%
Mumbai	2.47%
Delhi	2.33%

In Taipei, you can rent out a $1 million apartment for just $1,158 a month! If that does not scream speculation what does? Asian Financial Crisis II? A collapse of currency valuations across Asia will be a given in the next economic downturn.

When the next economic storm arrives at Asia's doorstep, how will central banks across Asia react? I would say that many central banks across Asia will be forced to significantly raise interest rates. Singapore, Thailand, Malaysia, Taiwan, and South Korea are the nations that will feel the full brunt of a currency crisis. And the individuals in these countries who are hedged with $USD or gold will not feel the direct impact that the broad majority of the populations of these countries will feel. Asia has had an extraordinary boom era, but it too will experience an overwhelming bust era.

In Canada, it would be easy to say that this country has pretty much the same problem as Australia. It made a big bet on housing on the back of never-ending Chinese prosperity. Real estate in Vancouver has similar house price-to-income ratios as does Sydney.

House Price-to-Income Ratio	Median Household Income	Median House Price & Income Ratio
Seattle	$66,900	$354,700 (5.3x)
Vancouver	$65,000	$670,000 (10.3x)

I find it laughable that a city like Vancouver (as beautiful as it is) has a median property price nearly twice as high as one of America's most expensive real estate markets. For a median house, Vancouver residents pay nearly twice the price that people do a three-hour drive down the road in Seattle. Seattle is a major business hub with the likes of Microsoft, Boeing, and Amazon! But just like in Australia, insanely high levels of household debt is a pretty good signal that Canada has one big IZNOP that will sooner than later break-down.

Country	Household Debt-to-Income Ratio
Canada	164%
USA	105%

And as for the New Zealanders, they too adopted the exact same

IZNOP model as the Australians (*which major Australian banks helped fuel*). New Zealanders too think that a new world has arrived on the back of rising real estate prices, alongside Chinese demand for lamb, wool, and other agricultural goods. Unfortunately for the Kiwis, shearing sheep and flipping houses is not a sustainable economic model.

So while Europe, Japan, and America have been trying to solve their problems from the moment their IZNOP models broke down, countries such as Australia, Canada, and Brazil have been taking on the same risk model that will inevitably leave them with the same challenges that the QE nations have experienced. I leave it to the notion that history has a good track record of repeating itself. It's simply too easy for a country to get highly stimulating GDP when you have a credit-fueled property bubble and a natural-resources boom. But as there are so many countries dependent on never-ending Chinese economic growth, I fear the global economy is in for one big economic shock that will leave countries that made this incredible bet on never-ending Chinese economic growth in economic ruins.

Chapter Fourteen

Stock Market Carnage

The Link Between East and West

First and foremost, we know that a lot of companies around the world have benefited significantly from the China growth story. We also know that a downturn in China will breakdown IZNOP business models in the emerging world, Asia, and Australia. It's a given that natural-resource companies and their suppliers are in the firing line of this potential economic storm. But how will many European and American companies weather the Chinese economic typhoon when its IZNOP model breaks down? Because, by all mathematical accounts, the stock market valuations of most American and European companies are today overvalued. And I think that the fault lines extending out from a Chinese economic meltdown would directly impact most industries around the world. Here are a few standout industries.

Luxury brands and the nouveau riche

For starters, how have luxury designer brands such Louis Vuitton, in the midst of Europe and America's large economic shock, continued to grow so strong? Because of a new wave of high-end luxury buyers from China and other parts of Asia. Let's face it, if you walked into a Louis Vuitton store in the U.S. and Europe back in 2005, you would have been lucky to have found an employee that spoke Mandarin.

Whether its Louis Vuitton, Christian Dior, Rolex, Cartier, or any other high-end luxury consumer brand, their stores worldwide are today very engaged to help the new-world buyers of their products. In other words, it is now more common than not that a small handful of employees in each and every store of these high-end consumer brands speak Mandarin or Cantonese. As I've walked through high-end luxury stores, I've found the majority of the Chinese buyers of high-end luxury goods to be a lot younger than one would assume would be able personally afford luxury items. When you speak to the employees of these luxury boutiques, particularly those workers who are hired to communicate with Chinese customers, they say that there are a lot of young Chinese between the ages of 20 to 30 years buying products in their stores. Between 20 and 30 years old! Now I know that there's always the occasional very successful individual under the age of 30 who has the financial means to spend $25,000 on a new wardrobe of clothes or a $30,000 watch from a major luxury brand. A very successful Hollywood actor or an individual who started a social media website with billions of users—those young, self-made, ultra-high-net-worth individuals do exist.

But if you take out the young tech and movie stars, I would say that there are a lot more young adults using mommy and daddy's credit card in these stores. Especially in Asia. That's the best conclusion I can come up with after my in-the-field research over the last two years. Furthermore, there's a lot of new-found wealth in this world that didn't exist several years ago. The Chinese have gone on a non-stop, high-end, luxury shopping spree that is showing signs of fading today. And the first thing that many nouveau riche want to do is to display their new wealth for the masses to see. So they go and buy the most expensive clothes, cars, watches, and boats in a relatively short period of time. Thus, luxury names have benefited significantly from the nouveau riche.

Car Maker	New Cars Sold 2009	Anticipated New Cars Sold 2014
Rolls Royce	1,002	4,000+

Today, the biggest market for many high-end luxury brands like Rolls Royce is China. For every 100 new Rolls Royce's sold by the manufacturer, 28 of them go to China.

The Chinese, and the residents of countries dependent on the China growth story with new-found wealth, love to buy high-end goods and services. But now there is what could only be described as one of the largest crackdowns on corruption in human history. The Chinese central government has taken a no-holds barred takedown approach toward corruption. And from the looks of it, it's starting to take its toll. Sales of high-end luxury watches in China have dropped by more than 27%. Prada, one of the world's biggest fashion names, recently saw profits fall by 24%! These are big hits aimed at the heart of an industry that significantly bucked the trend while Europe has been struggling. And in my opinion, it is an industry that will soon have to restructure and learn to once again earn off of old European, Middle Eastern, and American wealth rather than new-found wealth in China. Based on the affirmative actions of a central government, it seems the country now has the strong desire is to see its citizens enjoy the luxuries of life when they earn them the right way. Not the under-the-table way. And the central Chinese government must be commended for taking such a strong stance. It must not be easy. But this new generation of federal politicians don't seem afraid to clamp down on inequality through non-legit business activities. And high-end luxury brands will be the biggest loser of this continuous and proactive policy action.

Planes and Tourists

If you are a regular traveler to China, you know that traveling by air within China is a nightmare. The delays are awful. China may have some of the best barely used airport infrastructure on the ground, but in the skies there is limited airspace allocated to commercial jets, and long delays are a common feature. Additionally, airplane manufacturers such as Boeing and Airbus are now very dependent on China clogging up its skies even more with newly built commercial jets. But I fear that these airline manufacturers have made a very bad forecast on long-term sales of aircraft not only to China, but to the greater Asian region. Over the next 20 years in China alone, Boeing expects to sell more than 6,000 aircraft. The world's largest airline by passenger traffic, American Airlines, operates just 630 aircraft (prior to its merger with US Airways). Essentially, Boeing is forecasting that China will have the equivalent of several new American Airline's operating in China in the next 20 years. Minus some aircraft replacements, and a declining cost of fuel, I would say that Boeing and Airbus may find themselves right in the very heart of China's economic challenges when the IZNOP model breaks down. If Chinese airlines are to buy 6,000 aircraft over the next 20 years from Boeing alone, aircraft manufacturers are essentially forecasting that China will be a $77 trillion economy by 2027. So, if all those existing and future aircraft orders fall off the face of the earth, where will this leave the aviation industry?

It'll leave them with a lot of existing airplanes either sitting in a desert or being sold off at a steep discount. In 2008, the airline industry took an absolute beating. Although the price of fuel is unlikely to reach the soaring pre-GFC heights, the population on the ground in China may go completely spend-adverse. This will definitely impact passenger traffic numbers not just domestically within China, but internationally.

The knock-on effect of this would be huge. If the Chinese tourists numbers decline, so will the tourism dollars they bring with them. Particularly in Asia.

Country	Chinese Tourist Arrivals 2012 & annual growth (%) from previous year
South Korea	3.4 million (55%)
Thailand	2.8 million (62%)
Singapore	2.1 million (30%)
Japan	1.5 million (44%)
Malaysia	1.3 million (25%)

As you can see, the Chinese these days aren't shying away from taking international trips, and more Chinese than ever are traveling abroad. It's very similar to the part the Japanese played in regards to the Asian tourist boom before they went bust. American and European hotel chains such as the Marriot are investing very heavily into this market. There are 186 new properties earmarked to be opened by the Marriot Group over the next three years in Asia, but they may have to sell overnight stays for a much cheaper price if the China growth story comes to a halt. Because, like the Japanese in the early 1990s, the Chinese would stop taking as many holidays. And many international hoteliers would find themselves struggling. The same thing happened back in 2009. Starwood Hotels saw their stock price go from $74 in 2007 all the way down to $9.50 in 2009. But today the company has benefited significantly from the China growth story.

The overall carnage

Overall, I fear that many publically listed Western suppliers of goods and services that have made big bets on the China growth story will have to find alternative ways to profit in the future. Furthermore, a lot of corporate restructuring will have to take place. Survival for many companies will be tough. And many will go into receivership. In 1999 China was a $1 trillion economy, and by 2013 it was a $9 trillion economy. Somewhere in between those two numbers is a real economy and GDP number that will become China's future once their IZNOP model breaks down. So if a major company such as BMW rode the China growth story and then China fell backwards and became, say, a $7 trillion economy, how would that company handle it? Sooner than later this could be the global reality.

Many of these organizations that have made big bets on China will find themselves taking the biggest hits to their market capitalization. The knock-on effect of a China slowdown is huge. Even a company like Apple has $1 in every $7 of revenue generated coming from China. China is a very big market for Western companies across a very broad range of industries.

On the flipside, throughout this whole interconnected global mess you will find companies that would be able to benefit from a weakening China. The drop in the price of natural resources would make some private sector companies more profitable as the world becomes cheaper in $USD terms. For example, steel manufacturers in the United Kingdom and Europe would be able to acquire steel at a much cheaper price. And on top of that, as long as their products were providing enough value to customers, they would not need to drop the selling price so much. This drop in steel prices would give many companies in Europe and the U.S. that aren't dependent on China a lot of room to maneuver through a challenging time. But auto manufacturers that have been beneficiaries of the China growth story (such as BMW and Mercedes Benz) will struggle to sell as many cars as are being driven out of their factories.

Essentially, figuring out which companies will take the bigger hit will come down to the level of dependency and risk that each particular company has on the China growth story. The stock prices of iron ore miners in 2014 have been smashed. In Europe, I believe the German multinationals will be the biggest losers, as they have more skin in the game across a broad range of products and services geared towards the China growth story.

So, not only will German industry take a hit, its stock market (a very overvalued market) will inevitably be brought back to reality.

The double-barrel trigger to hit stocks

My conclusion regarding stock valuations today is that there's the risk caused by the excessive money printing (which isn't really helping economies get out of the danger zone), and there's the China risk. *When reality sets in that printing money doesn't work, it will hit stocks very very hard.* On top of this, if the very big IZNOP model in China breaks down, it too would send stocks tumbling around the world. This is the critical link between the high-risk growth model that China has adopted and its potentially punishing impact on the West. To intensify the situation, the failure of money printing in Europe, Japan, and America and the breakdown of China's IZNOP model are triggers for each other. In other words, a breakdown of China's IZNOP model could hit Europe, Japan, and, to a lesser extent, American stocks pretty hard. On the flipside, the failed economic policies of Europe, Japan, and America are enough to break down China's IZNOP model. Either way the impact will act like a domino effect and fiscally crush nations that made a huge bet on never-ending Chinese economic growth. And central bankers from the commodity club of nations will wonder how they got their economic forecasting on China so wrong. The simple answer for these central bankers in Australia, Brazil, Canada, etc., is this: When you're making an important long-term forecast regarding the amount of natural resources China will consume over the next decade or so, *pick up a calculator*!

It will be very interesting to see whose economic model breaks down whose. But the money printing and China risk factors, in my opinion, will be the contributing factors to the next global stock market crash. Let's face it, who wants to own stock in mining or luxury brands when China sneezes? And as money printing pushed stocks artificially high while offering minimal dividends to mom and pop investors, these same investors won't be clamoring to invest in the stock market when it's tumbling fast and still offering small dividends—or even losses. Neither will institutional investors want to invest when they realize that the value of many publically traded entities are actually worth nowhere near what they were valued in 2014.

It wouldn't surprise me if sometime before 2017 stock markets in Europe, America, and Japan fall by at least 50%. And, in my opinion, as much pain as it would cause, it would be for the better. Stock markets around the world simply can't continue to climb they way they have. They are overvalued. The bigger the risk, the bigger the fall. And when the next real fall comes, it will become very clear that the world has misjudged what the fair value of what a publically traded asset should actually be. Today, stocks are worth a lot more than what they should be worth. And they've been prime contributors to the lackluster economic growth in the countries that have already witnessed the breakdown of their IZNOP models.

Cash and Gold

As the global economic ship sails into this financial hurricane, two asset classes in particular will be the prime safe havens. They are the United States Dollar . . . and Gold.

If 2008 was anything to go by, we know that even if the U.S economy falls off a cliff, global investors rush to get their hands on the global reserve currency. The $USD is by far the easiest currency in the world to trade/exchange. And it's by far the one currency that would hold strong against every other currency in the world when the next major economic downturn hits this planet. If the global economy is hitting rock bottom, in which paper currency would you want to be holding *your* assets? Unless some bizarrely unique circumstance finds America with a monetary problem that somehow doesn't impact the rest of the global economy one bit, the $USD is the paper currency most global investors would want to be holding in a period of economic calamity. Why would global investors rush to the Brazilian Real or Australian dollar if the commodity markets and their IZNOP business models are collapsing? Does the Russian ruble sound like a safe bet? Will the European euro even exist in the next decade? Would you want to hold a diverse currency portfolio of Asian currencies when the Chinese property market bursts? Or would you rather hold the $USD in a major American or Swiss bank that has more cash on hand relative to the size of their operations when compared most other global banks?? This currency has a good track record of always holding up against all currencies around the world in periods of economic calamity?

Based on my research, a major global currency crisis is on the way. And against the $USD, many currencies around the world will take some very big hits, and central bankers will have to send interest rates skyward. It's very possible that there will be 40% to 80% drops in currency valuations in a broad host of countries. But gold, like the $USD, should hold value. Even if the value of gold declines in $USD terms, the value of gold against many currencies will increase in value. And, like the $USD, gold is easily tradable. In the absolute worst case, *which some well-known bears have supported with some excellent arguments,* the global monetary policy could one day revolve around the gold standard.

Although possible, I don't believe in this day and age that the gold standard will return. But if it does, the transition wouldn't be easy for anyone—*unless you are holding a lot of gold*. The gold standard is by far the world's last resort should the value of paper money in America simply become worthless. If the Brazilian Real or Australian dollar fall by 70% and 50% respectively, would the Fed start to use the gold standard? In my opinion, no. But if it's own currency, the global reserve currency, were to become worthless (as it did in Zimbabwe) because of the Fed trying to print its way out of a structural problem that doesn't require printed money, the gold standard would be the only option to keep the peace. So when a central bank decides to print more money in the future to buy up assets rather than pay down government debt obligations, it should take the Zimbabwean model into consideration. The Zimbabwean model is a clear example of what happens when money printing gets out of control to such an extent that interest rates rise to a billion-trillion percent. And what did Zimbabwe do to stop hyperinflation? It abandoned its own currency. So much for printing your way out of a problem!

Chapter Fifteen

Recommendations and Concluding Summary

Following the next global downturn—one that would be caused by central banks around the world—maybe we as a global society, and our financial regulators, can implement changes so that one day the world of economics once again makes sense to us all.

My research shows me that the global economy has now set the course for a very big economic kick in the guts. There will be pain, whether it be felt by a U.S. institutional investor who thought stocks would forever rise on the back of money printing, or the uneducated Australian homebuyer with an $800k loan living paycheck to paycheck. What I believe the next economic downturn will do is lay accountability squarely on the central bankers of the world. And this would not be a bad thing! Because society would then forever hold central bankers and their governments more accountable for their actions. Janet Yellen, Mario Draghi, and Haruhiko Kuroda may not have held their posts when all this financial mess started, but they are paid to do a job. And they need to be held accountable for their actions. If something like the *money-printing heroin shot* isn't working and these central bank leaders continue to print money and buy up assets, their governments and citizens should be asking some pretty tough questions.

Following the next economic downturn—which, on a global scale, should be worse than the GFC—we need to put into place rules and regulations ensuring that countries keep their economic models lean and, just as importantly, cyclic. It should be okay for a country to experience a recession from time to time; recessions clean out the excessive risk taking and force companies to innovate. And, just as importantly, a central bank should never let its economy get caught up in an IZNOP model. Never! *The IZNOP business model is why we have all these fiscal problems in the first place.*

Recommendation One

The 30-10-30 Plan

My first recommendation is designed to help countries never get caught up in the worst of asset bubbles in the very first place: *a credit-fueled property bubble.* And we know, these IZNOP business models have a 100% track record of failure, and they just need a trigger to send an economy crashing back to earth. No country or central banker can outsmart or outplay an IZNOP business model. That's what history and the laws of economics tell us. When these credit-fueled property bubbles burst they always crush the banking system that fueled the IZNOP model and leave a population confused because they thought "this time it was different."

My 30-10-30 plan is a plan that can be universally adopted and easily regulated. Many influential economic commentators, such as Stanford economics professor Anat Admati, are arguing that banks need to hold a lot more capital than they currently hold. When banks hold more capital, it generally means they are taking less risk. Who wants to hold their money in a bank that takes excessive risk? Unfortunately, many banks around the world hold very little capital against the risks they have undertaken. Australian banks are a very clear example. This leaves them very vulnerable to economic downturns, particularly when it comes to credit-fueled property bubbles. Banks around the world that take excessive risks don't like to hear that they should hold more capital, because it means that they make less profit when times are good, which affects the market capitalization of the bank. But banks also expect their central bank and government to be there to bail them out when the crap hits the fan. The less risk the banks take, the less chance there is that an economy will get caught up in an IZNOP business model. *In addition, there is less risk that a bank, or banking system, will require a bailout or go bust!*

My 30-10-30 plan can also organically force banks that lend to homebuyers to hold more capital across the board. And my 30-10-30 plan helps to provide enough buffer to the banks' risk profiles when they lend to homebuyers. In other words, it helps to build sustainable foundations between lender and borrower.

30-10-30

The first part of the plan is that homebuyers may not borrow more than 70% of the purchase price of a property. A homebuyer must come up with a 30% deposit or greater. This is the cut-off line. *No exceptions!* For example, if a homebuyer wants to purchase a $150,000 house, he needs to come up with the first $50,000 as a deposit for the home. This gives the bank that lends to a homebuyer a lot of breathing space between the value of the property at the date of purchase versus any economic instabilities that may arise in the future.

As an example, the homebuyer purchases the $150,000 home and loses his job in the midst of an economic downturn. Because every other buyer also had to come up with at least 30% deposit for their purchases, even if the property market were to fall by 30%, the banking system would still not be put in as bad a situations as the American or Irish banks back in 2009. These situations came about because a lot of homebuyers only provided a 5% to 20% deposit to purchase a home, and the property market got caught up in the IZNOP model and property prices fell, the damage was already done. A 30% deposit or greater with no exceptions is an effective enough buffer to stop homebuyers and lenders taking on excessive risks.

30-**10**-30

The second part of the 30-10-30 plan is that homebuyers who take a loan must hold in an account the equivalent of 10 months mortgage repayments. And for arguments sake, this could be held by the bank as its own Tier 1 capital until the loan is fully repaid. These funds must come from the homebuyer's income. *Nothing else.* Not a gift from parents, not a wedding gift, not casino winnings, etc. The homebuyer cannot touch this money and it generates interest while the money is held by the loaning bank. As the homebuyer's loan comes close to being fully repaid, the last mortgage repayment the homebuyer makes will be the 10 months worth of mortgage repayments that was deposited, on top of all the interest earned. This should dramatically cut down the overall time it takes a homebuyer to pay his or her home loan.

If, for whatever reason, the homebuyer suddenly is unable to pay mortgage repayments at a particular time of hardship, the bank will extract funds equivalent to the monthly mortgage repayment from the particular account holding the 10-months' worth of mortgage repayments. Once again, this reduces the bank's risk on the mortgage made, and it also provides a buffer for the homebuyer to get his or her act together. It's a win/win for both lender and borrower. As an example, if the homebuyer lost her job, she wouldn't need to offload her property right away. She would have enough time to find another job and income source. Wouldn't that have come in handy for Irish banks in 2009! And if the homebuyer can't find a way to resume making mortgage repayments after 10 months without a job, well, that's when the home enters receivership. But this strategy buys both parties a lot of time. And in most economic downturns, more time is by far the hardest commodity to find.

As a clear example:
If a homebuyer were to purchase a $150,000 home with a $50,000 deposit. The home loan would come to $100,000. In the first year, the monthly repayment on a 10-year loan that charges 10% interest is $1,666. Therefore to secure the loan, the homebuyer must deposit $16,666 into a holding account he cannot touch. The only reason this account can be touched is if the bank needs to take monthly mortgage repayment installments out of this account if the homebuyer is experiencing financial hardship. As the sum value of the loan becomes smaller as it gets paid off, these held funds will be able to make repayments for a prolonged period of time. I.e., five years into the mortgage repayments, the homebuyer still owes the bank $50,000 and is still paying 10% interest. That means this buffer should last 20 months in a period of financial hardship.

Overall, I believe this holding of funds that are equivalent to 10 months of mortgage repayments would be a good way to helping both the bank and borrower from getting themselves into a financial mess. It's also an important tool to prevent a property market from getting caught up in an IZNOP model. And I make a fair argument that the bank could hold this equivalent of 10 months of mortgage repayment to be classified as Tier 1 capital until the loan is fully paid.

30-10-**30**

The third part of the 30-10-30 plan is that homebuyers aren't allowed to spend more than 30% of their after-tax monthly household income on their mortgage in the first 12 months. Furthermore, a bank cannot lend a homebuyer a sum of debt that would mean that they would have to spend more than 30% of their income on mortgage repayments. This is important for many reasons.

Firstly, this protects the banking system from lending to homebuyers who have very generous parents willing to take excessive risks on their children's home purchase. As an example, in Australia parents come up with massive deposits for a home for their middle-aged kids, and still their children are stuck paying more than 50% of their incomes on mortgage repayments in a record low-interest-rate environment.

Secondly, it assures that regardless of what a household earns, the homebuyer will still be able to spend the greater proportion of his income on the greater economy outside of real estate. If a homebuyer is thick in an IZNOP model, he is exhausting so much of his income (prior to possibly losing his job) on mortgage repayments, that he, and his lender, are contributors to the break down of the IZNOP model. All it takes is for him to lose his job!

Thirdly? It just makes common sense! Nobody should live in a home and feel like they cannot enjoy life and spend some money outside of that home. And if interest rates rise, well, there's a big buffer compared to the household members that already spend 60% of their disposable incomes on mortgage repayments and then have to pay more when interest rates rise.

The overall benefits

There are so many external benefits to the 30-10-30 plan. It's also a plan that doesn't impede on property developers, construction, and property investor activity. In fact, it would offer property investors a much better annual gross rental yield. Because the 30-10-30 plan stops the property market from finding its way into an IZNOP model, it means less overall risk is taken for purchasers.

In November 2014, look at how much it cost property investors in Houston, Texas, and Melbourne, Australia, to purchase an investment property that would earn $30,000 in gross rental yield. It's not hard to guess which city is caught up in an IZNOP.

City	House Price to attain $30k gross rental income
Houston	$218,978
Melbourne	$722,891

As you can see, the common property investor in Houston is earning the same in gross rental income as the Melbourne property investor, but spending $500,000 less! If a Houston property investor spent $722,891 on three investments properties, the investor would be getting back almost $100,000 a year in gross rent. With my 30-10-30 plan, there's no way that the Melbourne property market would ever be able to get as overly priced as it has in the first place, which would allow for property investors to earn a much better yield on their property and monthly incomes!! *Not just a monthly losing tax write-off while in pursuit of capital gain!* And believe me, when the credit-fueled Australian property bubble bursts, some great jokes could be made if the problem wasn't so grave.

Today, the American property market is probably the market that could adopt the 30-10-30 plan with minimal impact on its economy. Property across the country (apart from a very small handful of major cities) is relatively affordable when compared to many overseas First World countries. And I truly hope this 30-10-30 plan is explored by banking regulators and central banks around the world.

There are simply too many instances wherein too much risk is taken by both the lenders and borrowers and property markets get caught up in IZNOP business models. America saw a stock market crash in the late '80s and early 2000s, as well as in 2008/9. But the last crash was the worst on the back of a credit-fueled property bubble bursting. Japan's credit-fueled property bubble burst and it was all over for them. So why do global economic regulators allow for these IZNOP models to happen in the first place, now that we know what the end result is?

The 30-10-30 plan is the regulator's best friend when it comes to protecting an economy from going anywhere near the worst of economic edges. But unfortunately, it's too late for countries like China and Australia. Their IZNOPs will burst. But hopefully, in the future, their governments will never let property prices get so far out of reach through the use of toxic credit again! Let's never forget, buying a home is more often than not the largest investment an individual will make in a lifetime. And it is the single asset class that can put the neck of any economy under the guillotine's blade.

Recommendation Two

Raise the minimum interest rate to 4% by 2017

Now that we have a solution to stop countries from getting themselves into catastrophic economic messes in the first place, the solution to solving countries' problems following a breakdown of an IZNOP business model is to get interest rates back up to a level where they can move cyclically in line with economic performance. In my opinion, this means that a 4% interest rate should become the new 0%. In this way, when an economy is grappling with all the debt problems, bank depositors and retirees can still earn income from the money the banking system is making a profit from. This stops those who've been responsibly saving from getting burned at the hands of an IZNOP model breakdown. History has a good track record of showing how an economy rebounds with a higher interest rate than with an interest rate at, or near, zero. If I'm wrong here, why aren't Japan and Europe booming today? Why did America rebound without QE in the early 1990s?

Banks have had a free ride over the last few years, and it simply has not brought the northern hemisphere's economy back to normal. In my opinion, a huge injustice has been served. If I deposit money into a European bank, I will get no interest. But the bank can lend the money I deposit into my bank account to someone else for a profit. That is *not* how the banking system should work.

Over the next two years, the BOJ, the ECB, the Fed, and the Bank of England should shift interest rates upwards with a target of 4% by late 2017. And so should every other central bank that has an interest rate of less than 4%. By the end of 2019, the target should be an interest rate of 8%. At first sight, it might sound crazy for the Fed, the ECB, and the BOJ to have interest rates of 8% by 2019. But these countries need to get as many retirees as they can living within their own means and off the pension. This will save governments an absolute fortune.

By no means would this structural shift in economic policy be a walk in the park. IZNOP business models that exist today will break down and investors hooked on the money-printing drug will suffer significantly. But we can't continue to live in a world where central bankers don't have a backbone and print money to feed an addiction to capital gain, which has starved the world of income. These powerful individuals—the central bankers—need to be the drivers of structural reform rather than economic drug dealers.

Rising interest rates will force governments to get their spending problems solved, and solved quickly! There are now 24-year-old Japanese citizens who don't know, or aren't old enough to remember, what it's like to have an interest rate higher than 1%! In the last two decades, the BOJ has never meaningfully tried to raise the interest rate to a point where it's people can earn money from deposits.

This strategy to raise interest rates would, for a period of time, cause global deflation in $USD terms, and almost all economies around the world would go into recession. But the world needs to become a cheaper place to live. Because asset inflation is through the roof! And the value of global assets needs to depreciate in order for them to become affordable again. Raising interest rates is the only way for this to happen. As long as the masses earn little or no income through interest or dividends, we shouldn't expect those same masses to spend more.

As far as I'm concerned, the younger generations of Japanese and Europeans now look forward to paying a hefty percentage of their incomes in tax to their governments to pay for the retirements of others. There is such a simple alternative: give the opportunity to retirees who have saved money to profit from their savings! They would be living better lives than they would if they were on the pension. Although my solution would inflict a significant amount of pain over the short term, it solves the very long-term structural problem that many countries with an aging population have not bothered solve. QE does not solve structural problems. It makes them worse!

Pay down government debt, don't buy it

The BOJ, the ECB, and the Fed have been printing trillions of dollars to buy government debt. Instead, the central banks should've been printing money over the last several years to *pay down* government debts/bonds. I'm not talking about trillions, but I am talking about just enough to make a small impact that would neutralize the impact of rising interest rates. *E.g., printing the equivalent of 1% to 2% of GDP to pay down government debt.* That's the only way that central banks can print money without getting investors hooked on financial heroin.

This would essentially be an off-balance-sheet investment by central banks, because you'd never see that money again when you'd pay down someone else's debt. But governments need to simultaneously produce a surplus (an pay down debt with the surplus) in order for this strategy to work. And if political leaders are too lazy to pull up their sleeves and reduce government expenditure the right way by finding where money is simply being burned into thin air, this would mean serious austerity measures. That's the easy, but very unjust way. But then again, austerity for a prolonged period of time has not panned out so well for the Greeks under a monetary union. Either way, the cost of assets would start to depreciate following the next economic downturn. But, on the positive side, the end result would be that more money would eventually start to flow into the real economy. And bonds once again would become a more affordable asset class for mom and pop investors wherein fair dividends would be given for allowing the government to borrow their smaller sums of money required.

Governments around the world need to start living within their means. If, by the year 2020, the PIIGS and France are still trying to borrow their ways out of their debt problems, sooner rather than later their governments will go bankrupt. But alternatively, bankruptcy may be the only way to force or allow the governments of these countries to restructure their finances. That could be a quicker and more proactive approach. A fresh start! And bankruptcy could possibly be a much better option than austerity. Particularly for Eurozone nations who are up to their noses in debt.

Look at Japan. Since 1987 its government has literally borrowed the equivalent of 150% of GDP to avoid bankruptcy! How is that working for Japan today? It's not! And it hasn't for the last 20-plus years! The Japanese government should've just declared bankruptcy back in 1997 and started fresh. Is the ECB going to spend the equivalent of 60% of EU GDP between now and 2020 to stop Eurozone nations from going into bankruptcy? Either governments of the PIIGS and France live within their own means with a very small amount of help from the ECB to pay down debt, or they should declare bankruptcy. In my opinion, either of those choices are better than the ECB buying debt for an infinite period of time. Why go the route of Japan?

It won't surprise me if one of the PIIGS states, such as Greece, one day opts to pull out of the Euro and/or declare bankruptcy. There is little evidence to suggest that the Greek government would ever be able to honor its existing debt obligations. In my opinion, Greece going back to the Drachma wouldn't be a bad thing. Having the ability to dictate its own monetary policy would probably help solve a lot of structural fiscal problems in Greece. And its Drachma would probably be undervalued for a long time, which is good for Greek exports and tourism. Although there would be a period of serious economic pain, the Greeks have been suffering for the last several years under the Euro anyway. Today, being part of the monetary union is simply not helping Greece. It would definitely be an interesting test case to see how bankruptcy would work out. If it does work for the Greeks, expect other countries to follow suit. As far as I'm aware, the Greeks don't like being told how to run their economy by the Germans, and the Germans don't like to keep flipping the debt bill for the Greeks. Should both these governments just walk away from each others problems? Because by now, German government bankers have hopefully pulled out a calculator and done the math. Either spend tens-of-billions of euros over the next couple of years continuously bailing out Greece again and again under harsh terms, or take the hit of never getting paid back by the Greeks and move on. Then again, Greece's debt problems would have never existed in the first place if Greece had been allowed to pay down its debt obligations with ECB printed money.

I cannot emphasize strongly enough how the central bankers (who have let interest rates fall to near zero) need to bring interest rates back to higher levels. The Fed, the ECB, and the

BOJ are digging their economies' graves if they continue down the path of zero interest. And the profit margin that a bank receives from standard bank accounts looks pretty unfair to me.

Share of profits from lending	Share of Profits
Lending Bank	99.5%-100%
Lending Bank's Standard Depositor	0-0.5%%

In my opinion, this is simply not a fair approach for bank deposit holders. Today in Japan and Europe, you deposit your money into a bank account that earns no interest and the bank loans out your money at a profit. You have absolutely no clue who's borrowing your money, nor do you know the risk profile of the person or corporation. Most banks in Europe will only offer you a little interest if you lock in your cash with the bank in a term deposit account. For example, the Portuguese bank Banco Esperito Santo will give you an interest rate of 1.50% if you put your money in a 12-month fixed-term deposit. So, if a Portuguese retiree with €100,000 of savings in cash put her money into a 12-month fixed-term deposit account at Banco Esperito Santo (*which failed an European Banking Authority's 2014 stress test*) she'd earn €28.87 per week of income. It's not easy to live in the Western world off that type of money. Hence, governments are forced to help out retirees a lot more than they should—because governments across Europe *can't live within their means*.

Concluding Summary

As I illustrated in the first chapter of this book, when a property market gets caught up in a credit-fueled IZNOP business model, all it takes is a trigger to bring that property market and banks that were fueling the fire to their knees. Additionally, innovative financial instruments such as junk CDOs were disasters in the making. The major ratings agencies of the world need to ensure that, beyond a shadow of a doubt, a AAA-rated financial instrument should in fact be the most fireproof investment that is on offer in the marketplace.

Political leaders and, more particularly, central bankers who become cheerleaders for flooding toxic sums of debt into a particular property market should've already learned from the past mistakes of other failed attempts to drive property prices at a rate that makes no economic sense. When wages aren't keeping up with a house price growth that is rising in sync with housing credit growth, alarm bells should be ringing . . . as this is the very early stage of an IZNOP model. And as history and the laws of economics tell us, the bigger the rise, the harder the fall. All credit-fueled property bubbles have ended in disaster. So why central bankers around the world don't spot these bubbles earlier on is simply beyond me—there are a wealth of resourceful tools, such as a simple calculator, to help make a fair assessment whether a property market is experiencing a credit-fueled property bubble. The only thing that credit-fueled property bubbles do for an economy is make a homebuyer feel richer for an intermediate period of time before the value of their homes collapse. This is what the citizens in countries such as Australia, China, Canada, New Zealand and many nations across Asia have to look forward to. The central bankers of these nations have simply let housing credit grow out of control.

The IZNOP business model has a 100% failure rate. It even broke down the American economy in 2008. It also took out Japan's economy and many nations across Europe. Since then, central bankers in Europe, America, and Japan have tried to take the easy but very dangerous way out of the fiscal mess that unfolded following the breakdown of their IZNOPs. Printing money and inflating particular asset classes has simply left us today with a lot of asset classes in bubble territory. And this was all done in the name of helping government's live beyond their means.

The end result? On the front end is a large proportion of retirees who should've been assets to an economy but who're today liabilities. Secondly, on the back end, you have an investment community hooked on fiscal heroin. The shot of morphine that the Fed gave the American economy over 2008-09 to alleviate the pain worked well. The shot was used at the appropriate time to alleviate significant pain. But since then, the American economy, the Main Street economy, without the help of the Fed, has picked itself back up off the ground and gotten itself out of one heck of a mess. But in the meantime, unfortunately, the Fed hooked the investment community on fiscal heroin, causing a large disconnect between the economic fundamentals and the value of stocks and bonds and the yields they deliver. Likewise for Japan and Europe. Printing money never solved America's structural problems. It never solved Europe's or Japan's problems either. The citizens of the PIIGS and France will see a lower standard in the quality of life. This leads to my conclusion;

Paying an abnormally high (inflated) price in asset investment equates to less money flowing through the real economy. Less money flowing through the real economy equates to deflation.

And in China, printing money has only laid the foundations of a future economic collapse that, by all accounts, should make the Japanese bust of the 1990s look like a walk in the park. Nevertheless, by no means will China be sent back into the stone age. This country will one day have the world's largest economy—once it has gone through one enormous deleveraging process. But it may never require the same volume of natural resources to fuel economic growth. And this will crush the commodity club of nations, particularly nations that produce iron ore. And their currencies will get crushed unless their central bankers raise interest rates. Either way, credit-fueled property bubbles around the world will burst.

I also sincerely hope that China aggressively tackles its environmental issues. China is truly an astonishing country. And to see clear Chinese skies day in and day out would be one of the greatest human achievements of the 21st century. And if any nation on earth has the manpower and the lack of red tape to make wonders happen, it's China.

Banks across America, Japan, and Europe offer measly returns, and retirees are forced to hack into their life savings much faster than they would if they were earning meaningful returns on the cash they entrust their banks to profit from. Just as bad, stock markets are overvalued simply because money printing turned the institutional investment community into capital gain junkies. There's too much evidence that suggests that stocks are rising and falling in line with money printing rather than with economic fundamentals.

When the next economic crisis comes knocking on planet Earth's door, it will be a hard one for many to escape. Non-American residents living off $USD and holding gold will probably weather the storm better than their neighbors who hold neither. Alongside failed bets on the China growth story, stock markets in Europe,

America, and Japan will be valued closer to what they were in 2009 than what they were in 2014. In my opinion, that wouldn't be a bad thing. When an asset bubble bursts, the value of assets become more affordable, allowing for more investors to make meaningful dividends. And the days of central bankers acting as fiscal heroin dealers will be over. Over the last few years, it has become pretty clear that institutional investors in Europe, Japan, and America have invested in stocks on the basis that their central bankers will continue to print money rather than based on the core fundamentals of an economy and future growth trends. And, as I clearly illustrate in the stock market chapter, there is an incredible impact on the value of stock markets when:

1. Money is printed.
2. Money printing is withdrawn.
3. Money printing is resumed.
4. Money printing is withdrawn in one economic superpower, but immediately accelerated in another economic superpower.

Following a global deleveraging event, I am confident that we as global citizens in a global economy will once again make investment decisions based on core fundamentals and data that tell us where the global economy is headed. The value of assets across the globe will become more affordable. And though structural spending problems exist in the United States, I strongly believe the world's largest economy will experience the least pain in the next economic downturn. But by no means am I saying America can avoid a recession by the end of 2017. The American economy may not be in the best shape of its life, but it is by far the very best of an incredibly bad bunch of economies that have a lot more structural problems. While the next generation of French are dreaming of becoming middle-class employees within one of the French government's heavily bureaucratic administrations, young Americans are dreaming of making something extraordinary of themselves. No need to second-guess where the majority of new innovation will come from for years to come. And innovation is something you can't print in a money-printing factory.

I am sincere in my hope that the contents of this book will help to spur the economic debate when it comes to money printing and credit-fueled property bubbles. More particularly, for the 99.9% of us who don't have a real voice in economic matters. I also hope that my two key recommendations are explored. Is it the right strategy for central bankers to print money to increase the debt burdens of the economies they manage? Should central bankers take more aggressive measures when there are early signals that an economy is experiencing a credit-fueled property bubble? These are the two questions that I believe aren't debated enough. And due to a lack of debate, we will only see history once again repeating itself.

Sources and Recommended Readings

For Australian's I would strongly recommend reading the following book by:
Philip Soos and Paul Egan
'*Bubble Economics: Australian Land Speculation 1830-2013*'
World Economic Association (2014)

US Interest Rate 1999-2007
http://www.tradingeconomics.com/united-states/interest-rate

Financial crisis timeline: Collapse and bailout
Polyana da Costa
Bankrate.com
http://www.bankrate.com/finance/federal-reserve/financial-crisis-timeline.aspx

'*In my opinion by far the best and simplest explanation on how the CDO market crashed*'
The Root Cause of the Financial Crisis: The CDO
Paddy Hirsch (February 22, 2014)
https://www.youtube.com/watch?v=jvLe2RN_qys

Bear Markets Are Inevitable
Bob Stokes
Elliot Wave International (18 March 2013)
http://www.elliottwave.com/freeupdates/archives/2013/03/18/Bear-Markets-Are-Inevitable.aspx#axzz3H99IflfI

Median and Average Sales Prices of New Homes Sold in United States
Census Bureau
http://www.census.gov/const/uspriceann.pdf

America's housing blackspots: Ten cities where property prices fell by up to 69% in FIVE YEARS
Daily Mail Reporter (12 May 2011)
http://www.dailymail.co.uk/news/article-1386006/Ten-cities-property-prices-fell-69-FIVE-YEARS.html

Monetary Policy and the Housing Bubble Figure Data
Finance and Economics Discussion Series 2009-49
The Federal Reserve Board
http://www.federalreserve.gov/pubs/feds/2009/200949/figure_data.html#figure1

The Hidden Killer
Revisiting the U.S. Housing Bubble
Political Calculations
Town Hall Finance (December 24, 2011)
http://finance.townhall.com/columnists/politicalcalculations/2011/12/24/revisiting_the_us_housing_bubble/page/full

Where should house prices be and how did they get so high?
Bergen Jersey Foreclosures (June 7, 2008)
http://www.bergenjerseyforeclosures.com/blog/info/entry/where_should_house_prices_really

Why was Japan Hit So Hard by the Global Financial Crisis
ADBI Institute
Masahiro Kawai & Shinji Takagi (October 2009)
http://www.adbi.org/files/2009.10.05.wp153.japan.gfc.pdf

Dr Housing Bubble. Charts by Gluskin Sheff & Havier Analytics
The Heisei Boom.
http://www.doctorhousingbubble.com/heisei-boom-financial-trickery-central-bank-voodoo-debt-federal-reserve-central-banks-too-big-to-fail-japan-us-bubbles/

Housing Markets in the United States and Japan: National Bureau of Economic Research
Edited by Yukio Noguchi & James M. Poterba (1994) University of Chicago Press
http://books.google.com.au/books?id=X37gyh4wajkC&pg=PA5&lpg=PA5&dq=japan+1980%27s+land+shortage&source=bl&ots=nPe1hPlu7Z&sig=PMb_RX7cwK5yL-ZM8m6cTszxa_o&hl=en&sa=X&ei=OXVZVPfMAuPdmAWf4IKwCA&redir_esc=y#v=onepage&q=japan%201980's%20land%20shortage&f=false

The Bubble Burst and Recession 1990s-
National Graduate Institute For Policy Studies.
http://www.grips.ac.jp/teacher/oono/hp/lecture_J/lec13.htm

Population Density Japan
http://www.infoplease.com/ipa/A0934666.html

Japan's property prices continue to rise.
Global Property Guide (May 15, 2014)
http://www.globalpropertyguide.com/Asia/japan/Price-History

Wheat from Chaff
Hussman Funds
Japan Stocks P/E Ratio Chart
John P. Hussman (December 1, 2008)
http://www.hussmanfunds.com/wmc/wmc081201.htm

Ponzi Scheme Definition
U.S. Securities and Exchange Commission
http://www.sec.gov/answers/ponzi.htm

Japan's Bubble Economy of the 1980's
The Bubble Bubble
Jesse Colombo (June 4 2012)
http://www.thebubblebubble.com/japan-bubble/

Recommended reading:
Harry Dent
The Demographic Cliff.
Schwartz Publishing (January 29,2013)
Please pay close attention to chapter 2 related to Japan. Pg 45-78

The mystery of Japan's Private Debt Levels (Solved?)
HBL *(blogger)*
Thought Offerings (September 22, 2009)
http://www.thoughtofferings.com/2009/09/mystery-of-japans-private-debt-levels.html

Japan unveils $275 billion stimulus package
Andrew Coen
Investment News (October 3, 2008)
http://www.investmentnews.com/article/20081030/REG/810309989

Quantitative Easing in Japan: past and Present
David Andolfatto & Li Li
Economic Synopsis, 2014, No 1 (January 10, 2014)
Federal Bank of St Louis
http://research.stlouisfed.org/publications/es/article/10024

Japan's Banking System: From the Bubble and Crisis to Reconstruction
Masahiro Kwai
PRI Discussion Paper (No. 03A-28)
Institute of Social Science, University of Tokyo Japan (December 2013)
Please review pages 4 & 25-30
https://www.mof.go.jp/pri/research/discussion_paper/ron080.pdf

Japan's Kaput?
Axel Merk (November 5, 2014)
SafeHaven Blog
http://www.safehaven.com/article/35681/japans-kaput

Abenomics Officially Leads Japan Into A Triple-Dip Recession – Weather Blamed; Nikkei Drops 600 Points, Back Below 17,000
Tyler Durden
ZeroHedge (November 16, 2014)
http://www.zerohedge.com/news/2014-11-16/abenomics-officially-leads-japan-triple-dip-recession

The Definition of Abenomics/ Abe's Arrows: A hit or miss?
Financial Times
http://lexicon.ft.com/Term?term=abenomics

Abe wants Pension Funds to Make 'Riskier Bets'
Pater Tenebrarum
ActingMan.com (May 21, 2014)
http://www.acting-man.com/?p=30667

UBS Bailout: Switzerland Bails Out UBS; Credit Suisse Raises Funds (Update 2)
Elena Logutenkova and Warren Giles
Bloomberg (October 16, 2008)
http://www.bloomberg.com/apps/news?pid=newsarchive&sid=aPHq_T5t4R9U

Swiss GDP Data
http://www.tradingeconomics.com/switzerland/gdp

P/E Ratios's: Is the Stock Market Cheap?
Doug Short
Advisor Perspectives (January 5 2015)
http://www.advisorperspectives.com/dshort/updates/PE-Ratios-and-Market-Valuation.php

Price-to-Earnings Ratio Chart (NYSE Arca)
Must –know: Has the bull run in global equities ended?
Russ Koesterich (November 11, 2014)
Market Realist
http://marketrealist.com/2014/11/why-you-should-invest-emerging-markets-now/

Countries not in recession during GFC
http://en.wikipedia.org/wiki/Timeline_of_the_Great_Recession

Examples of low dividends.
Dividend Yield for Stocks in the Dow Jones Industrial Average
Index ARB (2014)
http://indexarb.com/dividendYieldSorteddj.html

Federal Reserve Assets Chart & Historical Balance Sheet Data
EconDataUs (2014)
http://www.econdataus.com/fedbal.html

Australia Land Price Growth
Your Investment Property Magazine
Robin Christie (April 24, 2012)
http://www.yourinvestmentpropertymag.com.au/news/city-land-value-growth-the-best-and-worst-128412.aspx

Capital City Vacant Land Values Rise Through 2014
Street News (March 14, 2014)
http://www.streetnews.com.au/capital-city-vacant-land-values-rise-through-2014/

Will the Republican Majority Stop the Japanization of America
Forbes.com
Larry Macdonald (November 6, 2014)
http://www.forbes.com/sites/larrymcdonald/2014/11/06/will-the-republican-majority-stop-the-japanization-of-america/

1.8 Million U.S. Properties with Foreclosure Filings in 2012
RealtyTrac.com
RealtyTrac Staff (January 14, 2013)
http://www.realtytrac.com/content/news-and-opinion/2012-year-end-foreclosure-market-report-7547

Fault Lines – For Sale: The American Dream
Al-Jazeera Documentary
Al –Jazeera (2012)
https://www.youtube.com/watch?v=S3rzN42HE00

American Unemployment Rate Data
Tradingeconomics.com
http://www.tradingeconomics.com/united-states/unemployment-rate

American GDP Growth Rate Data
Tradingeconomics.com
http://www.tradingeconomics.com/united-states/gdp-growth

Is Australia's Welfare Spending Heading Down the Same Path as Europe's?
ABC Australia (FACTCHECK) (February 3, 2014)
http://www.abc.net.au/news/2014-02-03/kevin-andrews--makes-unfounded-welfare-claim/5215798

Irish House Price Growth Data
http://www.globalpropertyguide.com/Europe/ireland/Price-History

David McWilliams & Austin Hughes Debate on the Irish Housing Bubble
Prime Time Ireland (October 16, 2003)
RTE
https://www.youtube.com/watch?v=cxtkjZFfuZI

Morgan Kelly & Jim Power Debate on the Irish Housing Bubble
Prime Time Ireland (April 17, 2007)
RTE
https://www.youtube.com/watch?v=Gd6ZwqLePC0

Futureshock – Property Crash (Ireland)
Documentary by RTE Ireland (April 16, 2007)
https://www.youtube.com/watch?v=ZOE43_YnlOQ

Irish Net-Migration Data & Tables
http://emn.ie/emn/statistics

What Lies Beneath? Recent Trends in Irish Mortgage Arrears
Reamonn Lydon & Yvonne McCarthy
Central Bank of Ireland (November 2011)
http://www.centralbank.ie/publications/documents/14rt11.pdf

Europe's QE Quandry (ECB Balance Sheet)
Jana Randow
Bloomberg (revised article updated January 22,2015)
http://www.bloombergview.com/quicktake/europes-qe-quandary

Is the Eurozone Economy Being Dragged into a Deadly Spiral of Deflation?
Szu Ping Chan
The Telegraph (August 14, 2014)
http://www.telegraph.co.uk/finance/economics/11033550/Is-the-eurozone-being-dragged-into-deadly-spiral-of-deflation.html

ECB Fails 25 Banks as Italy Fares Worst in Stress Test
Jeff Black
Bloomberg (October 26, 2014)
http://www.bloomberg.com/news/2014-10-26/ecb-test-shows-25-billion-euro-capital-gap-at-euro-banks.html

Quantitative Easing in the United Kingdom
http://en.wikipedia.org/wiki/Quantitative_easing#United_Kingdom
Go Forth and Multiply London
Dan McCrum
FT Alphaville (February 17, 2014)
http://ftalphaville.ft.com/2014/02/17/1774432/go-forth-and-multiply-london-edition/

House Prices are Booming Again but the Bust That's Bound to Follow will Cost us Dear
David Blanchflower
The Independent (September 1, 2013)
http://www.independent.co.uk/voices/comment/house-prices-are-booming-again-but-the-bust-thats-bound-to-follow-will-cost-us-dear-8793316.html

Are Foreign Investors Really Buying Up All of London's Prime Properties
Colin Wiles
The Guardian (November 14, 2013)
http://www.theguardian.com/housing-network/2013/nov/14/london-property-foreign-investors

Real GDP Growth Rate Data (Europe)
Eurostat
http://epp.eurostat.ec.europa.eu/tgm/table.do?tab=table&init=1&plugin=1&language=en&pcode=tec00115

Up To 146 Million Risk Poverty if EU's Austerity Drags On
Video from RT (September 21, 2013)
http://rt.com/business/eu-poverty-oxfam-austerity-154/

Budget 2012: George Osborne Resolves That 'Britain Will Earn its Way Out of Trouble'
2012 Budget Coverage
The Telegraph (21 March 2012)
http://www.telegraph.co.uk/finance/budget/9158114/Budget-2012-George-Osborne-resolves-that-Britain-will-earn-its-way-out-of-trouble.html

China Stocks are Value
Roger Beattig
International Business Times (December, 3 2012)
http://www.ibtimes.com/china-stocks-are-value-915407

As China Opens Stock Market to Foreign Investors, Bargains Await Risk Takers
Wei Gu
Wall Street Journal (September 11, 2014)
http://online.wsj.com/articles/as-china-opens-stock-market-to-foreign-investors-bargains-await-risk-takers-1410471001

How to Get Chinese to Buy Stocks
Adam Minter
Bloomberg View (September 5, 2014)
http://www.bloombergview.com/articles/2014-09-05/how-to-get-chinese-to-buy-stocks

PBOC's $126 Billion No Rate-Cut Proxy for UBS: Chart of the Day
Kyoungwha Kim
Bloomberg Business (November 12, 2014)
http://www.bloomberg.com/news/2014-11-11/pboc-s-126-billion-no-rate-cut-proxy-for-ubs-chart-of-the-day.html

American Government Debt-to-GDP.
http://www.tradingeconomics.com/united-states/government-debt-to-gdp

Profits Without Prosperity
William Lazonick
Harvard Business Review ((September 2014 Issue)
https://hbr.org/2014/09/profits-without-prosperity

LVMH Shares Slump as Profit Miss Weighs on Luxury Stocks
Andrew Roberts
Bloomberg Business (July 25, 2014)
http://www.bloomberg.com/news/2014-07-24/lvmh-first-half-profit-trail-estimates-on-currencies-cognac.html

LVMH Stock Price/ Balance Sheet Data
https://au.finance.yahoo.com/q/is?s=MC.PA&annual

GE Stock Price/ Balance Sheet Data
https://au.finance.yahoo.com/q/bs?s=GE&annual

Japan Just Boosted QE And The Nikkei Exploded To A 7-Year High
Mike Bird
Business Insider (October 31, 2014)
http://www.businessinsider.com.au/japan-just-boosted-qe-and-the-nikkei-exploded-to-a-seven-year-high-2014-10

Japan Price to Earnings (ttm)
Vector Grader
http://www.vectorgrader.com/indicators/japan-price-earnings

Has the Magic of QE Finally Feded & Should Investors Take Defensive Action?
247Bull Editor
247Bull.com (October 26, 2014)
http://www.247bull.com/has-the-magic-of-qe-finally-faded-should-investors-take-defensive-action/

Bank Failures in the Major Trading Countries of the World: Causes and Remedies.
Benton E. Cup
Quarum Books (1998)
http://books.google.com.au/books?id=rnV3lsj5x4EC&pg=PA43&lpg=PA43&dq=the+netherlands+bank+failures&source=bl&ots=4Vk_M6pQ6Y&sig=PTzyMluauipj6uHV7d-OYCuQ2n8&hl=en&sa=X&ei=EzJsVNrBBpCrogTB24G4BA&redir_esc=y#v=onepage&q=the%20netherlands%20bank%20failures&f=false

France Has the Longest Retirement Age
Jessica Morris: OECD
CNBC (March 19, 2014)
http://www.cnbc.com/id/101507378#.

Dwelling Prices and Household Income
Ryan Fox and Richard Finlay
RBA Bulletin- (December Quarter 2012)
Reserve Bank of Australia
http://www.rba.gov.au/publications/bulletin/2012/dec/2.html

France's Age Structure
Index Mundi
http://www.indexmundi.com/france/age_structure.html

Francois Hollande's Popularity at Rock Bottom, But He Has No Intention of Quitting
John Lichfield
The Independent (18 September 2014)
http://www.independent.co.uk/news/world/europe/franois-hollandes-popularity-at-rock-bottom-but-he-has-no-intention-of-quitting-9742177.html

Gross Rental Yields- Japan compared to Continent
Global Property Guide (2013)
http://www.globalpropertyguide.com/Asia/japan/rent-yields

Household Debt (%) of Household Disposable Income Chart
Reserve Banks of Australia
http://www.rba.gov.au/speeches/2003/images/sp-gov-030403-graph1.gif

Historical GDP of China
http://en.wikipedia.org/wiki/Historical_GDP_of_the_People's_Republic_of_China

US Real GDP by Year
Multipl.com (2014)
http://www.multpl.com/us-gdp-inflation-adjusted/table

Country Comparison: Investment (Gross Fixed)
The World Factbook.
CIA
https://www.cia.gov/library/publications/the-world-factbook/rankorder/2185rank.html

China Has Consumed More Cement in 3.5 years than United States did in 100 Years says Bill Gates.
Hound Dog
Daily Kos (June 13, 2014)
http://www.dailykos.com/story/2014/06/13/1306854/-China-has-consumed-more-concrete-in-3-5-years-than-United-States-did-in-100-years-says-Bill-Gates

Housing Bubble in China?
Ankai Kenneth Mei
RBC Properties (February 7, 2013)
http://www.rbc-properties.com/housingbubbleinchina/

China in Transition
Henry H. Mcvey
KKR (April 9, 2013)
http://www.kkr.com/global-perspectives/publications/china-transition

Chinese Debt Worries and Growth
Shane Oliver
Oliver's Insights
AMP Capital (19 February, 2014)
http://www.ampcapital.com.au/article-detail?alias=/olivers-insights/february-2014/chinese-debt-worries-and-growth

Historic Inflation China- CPI Inflation
Inflation.eu
http://www.inflation.eu/inflation-rates/china/historic-inflation/cpi-inflation-china.aspx

China's Superbank is the Latest Bad Solution to the Country's Credit Addiction
Gwinn Guilford
Quartz (October 10, 2013)
http://qz.com/133588/chinas-superbank-is-the-latest-bad-solution-to-chinas-credit-addiction/

Is China About to Crack?
Marco Polo
Of Wealth (March 21, 2014)
http://www.ofwealth.com/is-china-about-to-crack/#.VHMdaUuFxvA

It's time for China to heed Global Competitiveness Reports
China Economic Review (May 22, 2014)
http://www.chinaeconomicreview.com/global-competitiveness-report-China-IMD-foreign-investment-appeal

China Also Tapers, Forced to Promptly Bail Out Money Markets
Tyler Durden
Zero Hedge (December 12, 2013)
http://www.zerohedge.com/news/2013-12-19/china-also-tapers-forced-promptly-bail-out-money-markets

Shanghai Composite Index Chart
CNBC
http://data.cnbc.com/quotes/.SSEC/tab/2

Historical Debt Outstanding – Annual 2000-2014
Treasury Direct
U.S. Department of the Treasury, Bureau of the Fiscal Service
http://www.treasurydirect.gov/govt/reports/pd/histdebt/histdebt_histo5.htm

Govt says mortgage purchase not a 'bailout'
Dana Robertson
ABC Australia (September 26,2008)
http://www.abc.net.au/lateline/content/2008/s2375777.htm

Australia's Housing Bubble is Real and Banks are to Blame, Says Author
Jonathan Shapiro
Sydney Morning Herald (August 28, 2014)
http://www.smh.com.au/business/the-economy/australias-housing-bubble-is-real-and-banks-are-to-blame-says-author-20140828-109ahx.html

Three Forces Pushing Australia Towards Recession
Callam Pickering
Business Spectator (July 23, 2014)
http://www.businessspectator.com.au/article/2014/7/23/australian-news/three-forces-pushing-australia-towards-recession

Population Density of Australia
http://en.wikipedia.org/wiki/Australia

The Greatest Economic Myth in Modern Western History
Lindsay David
Australia: Boom to Bust Blog (August 4, 2014)
http://blog.australiaboomtobust.com/2014/08/greatest-economic-myth-modern-western-history/

Median Property Prices Across Sydney Out of Control
Lindsay David
Australia: Boom to Bust Blog (August 24, 2014)
http://blog.australiaboomtobust.com/2014/08/median-property-prices-across-sydney-control/

10 Most Expensive Property Markets by M2
Lindsay David
Australia: Boom to Bust Blog (August 25, 2014)
http://blog.australiaboomtobust.com/2014/08/10-expensive-property-markets-m2/

10 Most Expensive Markets for Real Estate
Robert Frank
CNBC (March 5, 2014)
http://www.cnbc.com/id/101468652

Steve Keen and Christopher Joye Debate Australian Housing Bubble
Business Today
ABC Australia (February 14, 2011)
https://www.youtube.com/watch?v=-uHQeYY6K98

Tony Locantro 'Housing Bubble Trouble into 2015'
Tony Locantro
Sky Business Channel Australia
https://www.youtube.com/watch?v=r7KT952AmnI

Immigration Should Be Driving Up Rents
Lindsay David
Australia: Boom to Bust Blog (October 23, 2014)
http://blog.australiaboomtobust.com/2014/10/immigration-driving-rents/

'RBA Says Foreign Buyers not to Blame for Housing Shortage'
Rebecca Thistleton
Sydney Morning Herald (June 27, 2014)
http://www.smh.com.au/business/the-economy/rba-says-foreign-buyers-not-to-blame-for-housing-shortage-20140627-zsnzj.html

Australia- New Housing Starts Put California and Texas to Shame
Lindsay David
Australia: Boom to Bust Blog (October 20, 2014)
http://blog.australiaboomtobust.com/2014/10/australia-new-housing-starts-put-california-texas-shame/

Irrational Exuberance Down Under
William Pesek
Bloomberg View (September 22, 2014)
http://www.bloombergview.com/articles/2014-09-22/irrational-exuberance-down-under

Australian Treasurer: U.S Shutdown Taught us a Lesson (Joe Hockey Interview)
Interview by Amanda Drury (Written by Katie Holliday)
CNBC (October 14, 2013)
http://www.cnbc.com/id/101111726

Highly recommended website (Macrobusiness)
www.macrobusiness.com.au

Australia's Addiction to Private Debt
Philip Soos & Paul Egan
MacroBusiness (October 15, 2014)
http://www.macrobusiness.com.au/2014/10/australias-addiction-to-private-debt/

Investors Continue to Gorge on Mortgage Debt
Leith van Onselen (a.k.a The Unconventional Economist)
MacroBusiness (May 30, 2014)
http://www.macrobusiness.com.au/2014/05/investors-continue-to-gorge-on-mortgage-debt/

Interest Only Loans Australia's Subprime
David Llewellyn-Smith (a.k.a. Houses and Holes)
MacroBusiness (October 16, 2014)
http://www.macrobusiness.com.au/2014/10/interest-only-loans-are-australias-subprime/

The Great Housing Shortage Myth
Cameron Murray (a.k.a Rumplestatskin)
Macrobusiness
http://www.macrobusiness.com.au/2014/09/the-great-shortage-housing-myth/

Australian Outstanding Housing Credit Hits a Record $1.407T in October
David Scutt
Scutt Partners
http://www.scuttpartners.com.au/news/australian-outstanding-housing-credit-hits-record-1-407t-october/

The Propertied Federal Political Class
Lindsay David, Philip Soos, Paul Egan
Australia: Boom to Bust Blog (August 5, 2014)
http://blog.australiaboomtobust.com/2014/08/propertied-federal-political-class/

Bubble Economics: Australian Land Speculation 1830-2013'
Philip Soos and Paul Egan
World Economic Association (2014)
3.2.4 Bank Capital Ratios and Risk-Weighted Asset Methodology pp. 425-443

Australian Iron Ore Export Data
Australian Bureau of Statistics & Bloomberg
Bloomberg (2014)

Iron Ore Miners Adjust Break-evens
David Llewellyn-Smith (a.k.a. Houses and Holes)
MacroBusiness (September 8, 2014)
http://www.macrobusiness.com.au/2014/09/updated-iron-ore-miner-break-evens/

Rousseff's Second-Term Goal: Kick-Start Brazil Growth
Raymond Collit & Gerson Freitas Jr
November, 24, 2014
http://www.bloomberg.com/news/2014-11-24/rousseff-s-second-term-goal-kick-start-brazil-growth.html?hootPostID=c3b3e89ac6b795ad852808395367a070

10TH Annual Demographia International Housing Affordability Survey
Alan Bertaud
Demographia (January, 2014)
http://www.demographia.com

Household Debt to Income Ratio, USA vs Canada
Barry Ritholtz
The Big Picture
http://www.ritholtz.com/blog/2013/10/household-debt-to-income-ratio-usa-vs-canada/

BMW Worldwide Sales
http://en.wikipedia.org/wiki/BMW#Worldwide_sales

or

http://annual-report2012.bmwgroup.com/bmwgroup/annual/2012/gb/English/pdf/report2012.pdf

Rolls-Royce sees record 33% Boost in Luxury Car Sales
BBC News (July 8, 2014)
http://www.bbc.com/news/business-28209768

Apple Sales Growth Slips in China; iPhone 6 Delay Partly to Blame
Lance Whitney
CNET (October 21, 2014)
http://www.cnet.com/news/apple-sales-slip-in-china-due-to-regulatory-delay/

China Tops US as Rolls-Royce's Biggest Market
Colum Murphy
Wall Street Journal (January 10, 2014)
http://blogs.wsj.com/chinarealtime/2014/01/10/china-tops-u-s-as-rolls-royces-biggest-market/

Chinese Officials Rush to Sell Luxury Homes Amid Corruption Crackdown
Esther Fung & Alyssa Abkowitz

Wall Street Journal (August 17, 2014)
http://www.wsj.com/articles/chinese-officials-fearing-scrutiny-amid-a-crackdown-on-graft-rush-to-sell-luxury-homes-1408316680

China Targets Corruption, Luxury Brands Mourn
Evan Osnos
The New Yorker (February 7, 2013)
http://www.newyorker.com/news/evan-osnos/china-targets-corruption-luxury-brands-mourn

Boeing Expects Big Numbers in China
Ben Geier
Fortune Magazine (September 4, 2014)
http://fortune.com/2014/09/04/boeing-expects-big-numbers-in-china/

Largest Airlines in the World by Passengers Carried and Fleet Size
http://en.wikipedia.org/wiki/World%27s_largest_airlines#By_passengers_carried_.28millions.29

American Airlines Fleet (Data may change once US Airways planes included post-merger)
http://en.wikipedia.org/wiki/American_Airlines_fleet#Current_Fleet

25 Most Popular Destinations for Chinese Tourists.
Michelle Grant (Euromonitor)
SKIFT (September 3, 2013)
http://skift.com/2013/09/03/top-25-most-popular-destinations-for-chinese-tourists/

Marriot International Showcases Growth in Asia with the Addition of 186 Properties, Including Six New Luxury Hotels in October
Marriot News Center (October 15, 2013)
http://news.marriott.com/2013/10/marriott-international-showcases-growth-in-asia-with-the-addition-of-186-properties-including-six-ne.html

Japan Government Debt to GDP Ratio
Trading Economics
http://www.tradingeconomics.com/japan/government-debt-to-gdp

Como 'Zamparse' 5 Trilliones de Dolares…Asi…Sin Mas!!
Marcos Hofmann
Marcos H. Blog (March 25, 2013)
http://marcoshofmann.com/2013/06/25/como-zamparse-5-trillones-de-dolares-asi-sin-mas/

Big Banks a Bigger Risk Since GFC, Says US Expert Anat Admati.
Michael Bennet & Adam Creighton
The Australian (September 13, 2014)
http://www.theaustralian.com.au/business/financial-services/big-banks-a-bigger-risk-since-gfc-says-us-expert-anat-admati/story-fn91wd6x-1227057074328

Recommended Reading
Bankers, New Clothes
Anat Admati & Martin Hellwig
Princeton University Press (March 23, 2014)
http://bankersnewclothes.com

Disclaimer

The views and commentaries expressed on these pages reflect my personal views and opinion in my individual capacity. Any statements made in this book about persons or groups are only personal opinions and are not intended to be truthful factual representations nor disparagements of these persons or groups. In addition, please be duly informed that when comments are made about a past or present government policy, issue, or historical event, I am only relying on the publicly available facts and I have no personal knowledge of the facts or the merits of the issues on which I comment outside of what has been publicly published. I try my very best to understand the facts and other matters that I comment on, yet I would still strongly recommend that you should read these opinions and other sources again and judge them by yourself. The personal opinions I have formed in this book based on the research conducted are my personal views and does not constitute financial advice in any way, shape or form to the reader. If you seek financial advice I strongly suggest seeking financial advice from a professional financial advisor.

Regards
Lindsay David

www.ingramcontent.com/pod-product-compliance
Lightning Source LLC
Chambersburg PA
CBHW051646170526
45167CB00001B/348